Welcome to Club Senior!

By Phillip B. Fehrenbacher

Special thanks to my wife Julie
for her support in this endeavor
and putting up with me for 45 years!
And no, none of the cartoons in this
book represent either one of us...
or our relationship to each other!

Printed by CreateSpace, An Amazon.com Company

This publication is dedicated to all
men and women who have survived
illness, wars, natural disasters-
and raising children-
to reach retirement and finally
reap the benefit of their investments...
which may or may not be good news!

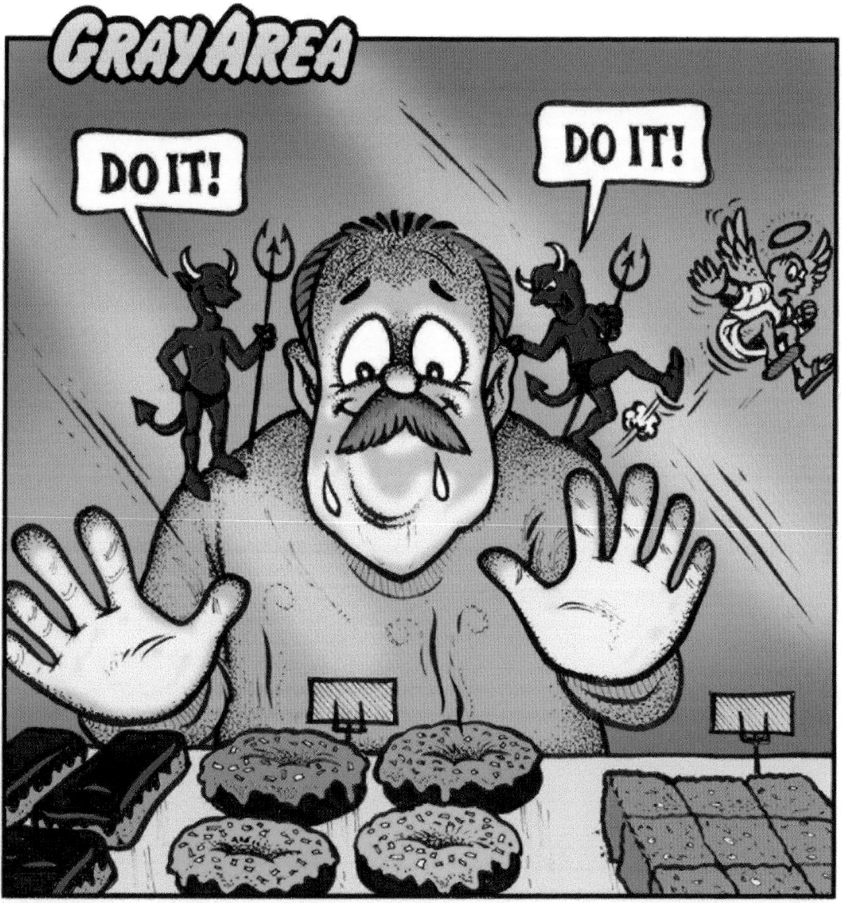
GRAY AREA
DO IT!
DO IT!

WHERE DECISIONS ARE EASIER TO MAKE!

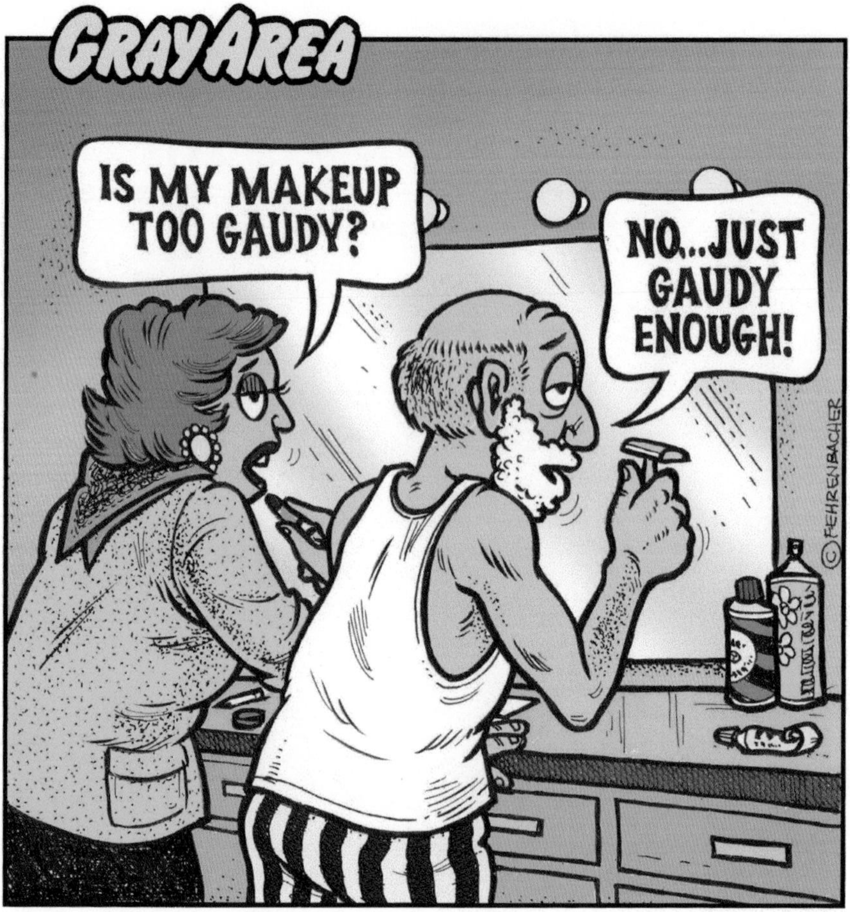
GRAY AREA
IS MY MAKEUP TOO GAUDY?
NO...JUST GAUDY ENOUGH!
© FEHRENBACHER

GRAY AREA
WELL, TECHNICALLY YES... YOU ARE HEIGHT/WEIGHT PROPORTIONATE, HOWEVER...
© FEHRENBACHER

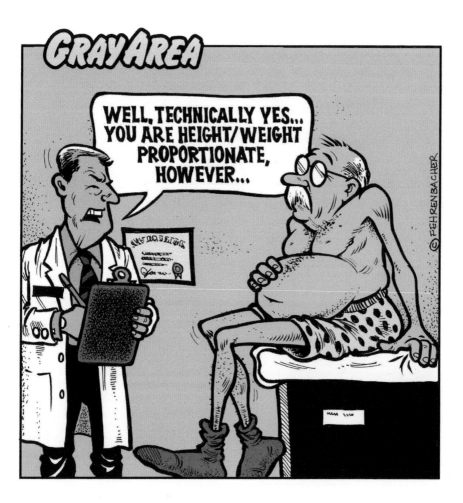

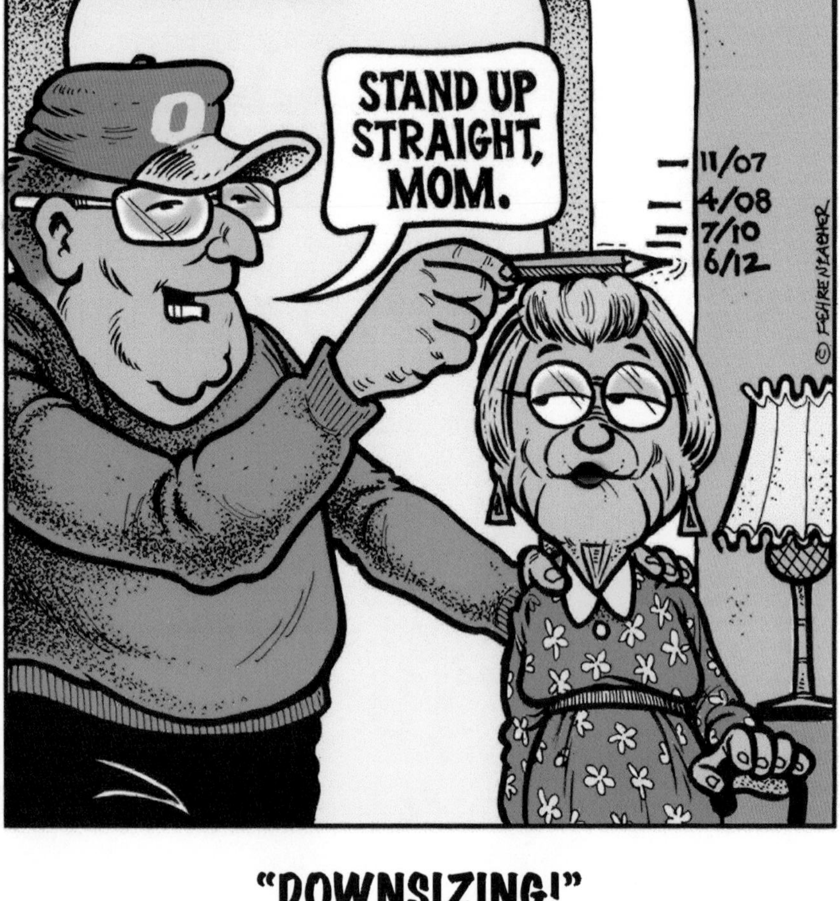
GRAY AREA
STAND UP STRAIGHT, MOM.
11/07
4/08
7/10
6/12
© FISHRENZACHER

"DOWNSIZING!"

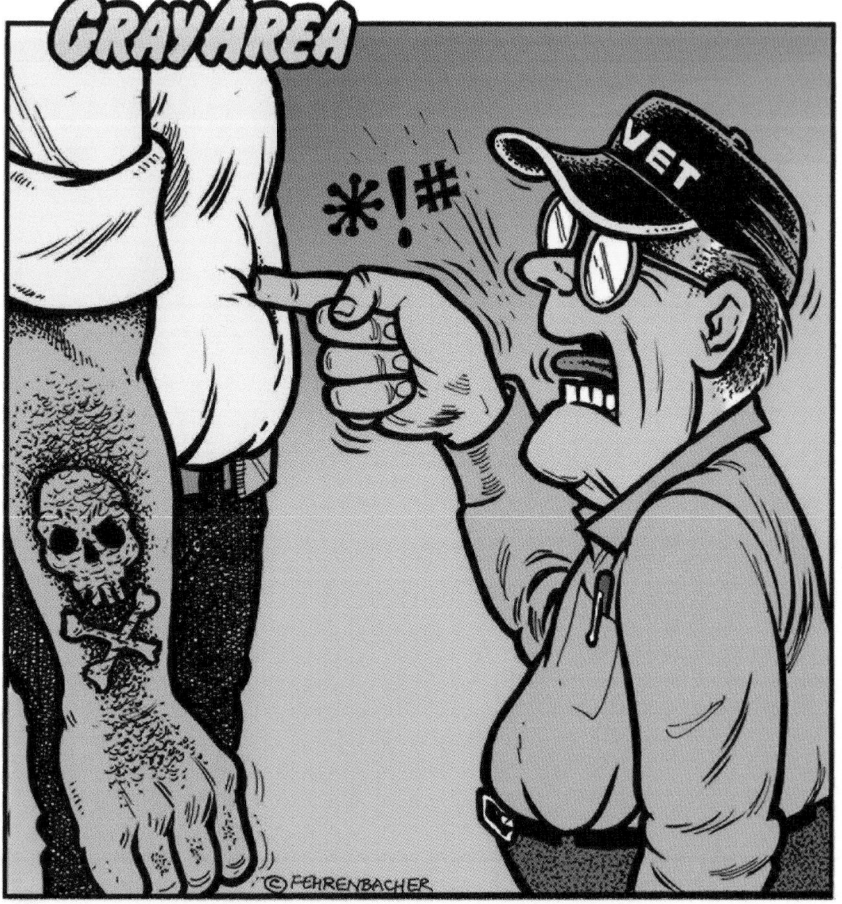
GRAY AREA
*!#
VET
© FEHRENBACHER

EARL FAILS THE FIGHT-OR-FLIGHT RESPONSE FOR SENIORS...BIG TIME!

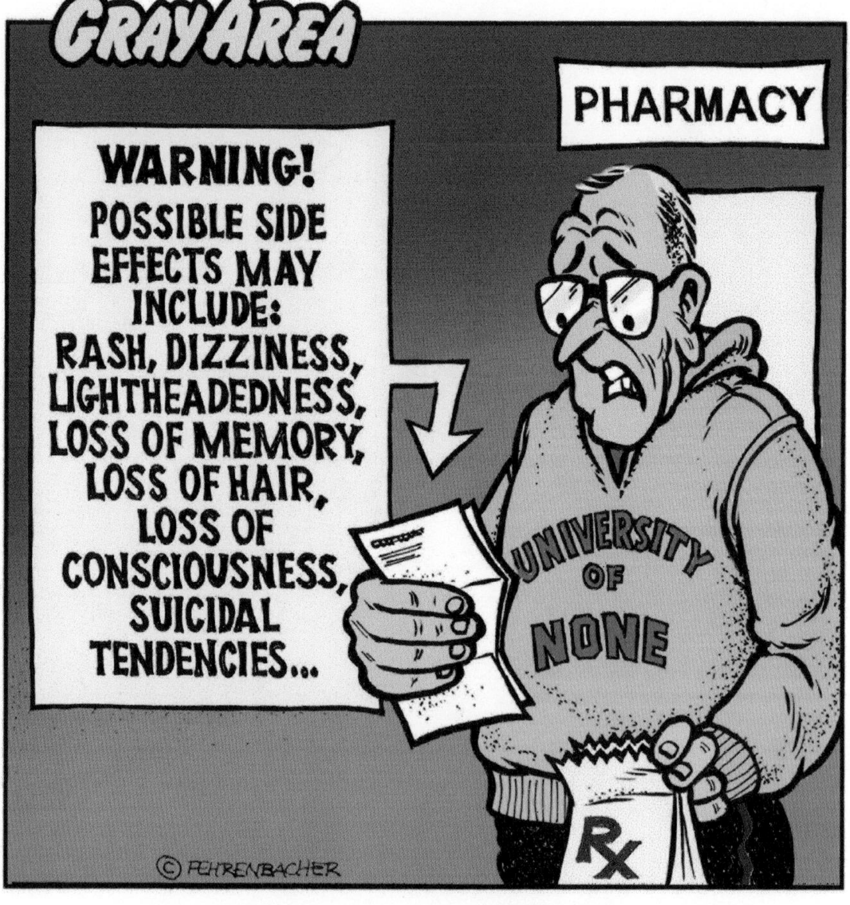
GRAY AREA
PHARMACY
WARNING!
POSSIBLE SIDE EFFECTS MAY INCLUDE:
RASH, DIZZINESS, LIGHTHEADEDNESS, LOSS OF MEMORY, LOSS OF HAIR, LOSS OF CONSCIOUSNESS, SUICIDAL TENDENCIES...
UNIVERSITY OF NONE
RX
© FEHRENBACHER

SO...WHAT'S THE DOWNSIDE?

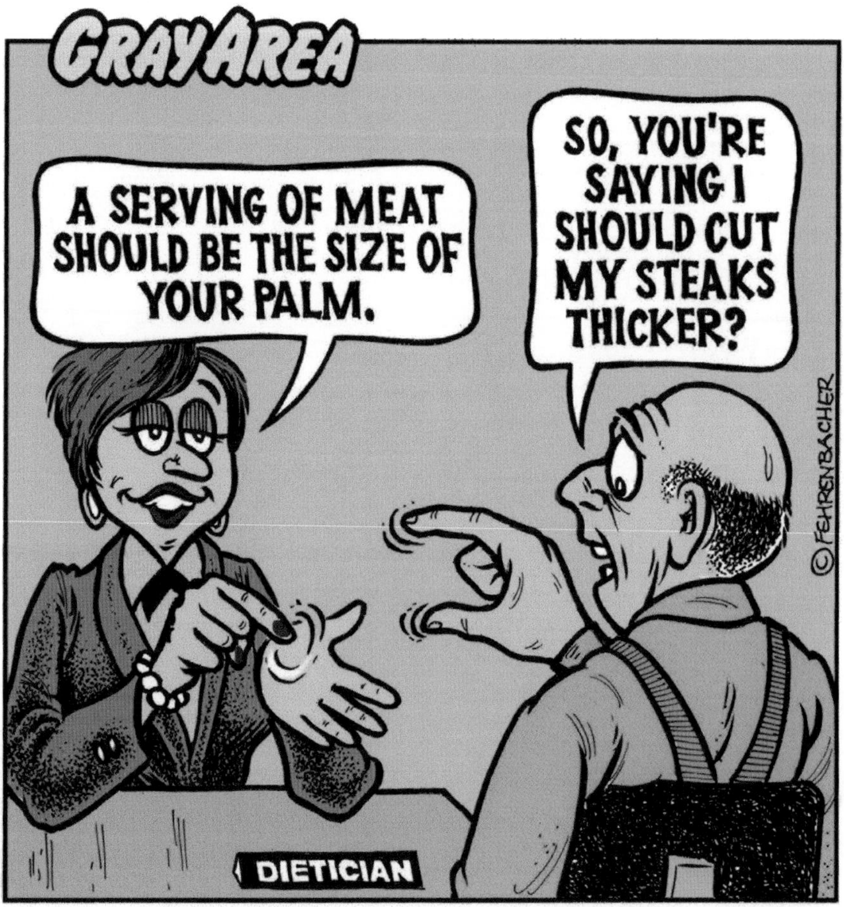
GRAY AREA
A SERVING OF MEAT SHOULD BE THE SIZE OF YOUR PALM.
SO, YOU'RE SAYING I SHOULD CUT MY STEAKS THICKER?
DIETICIAN
© FEHRENBACHER

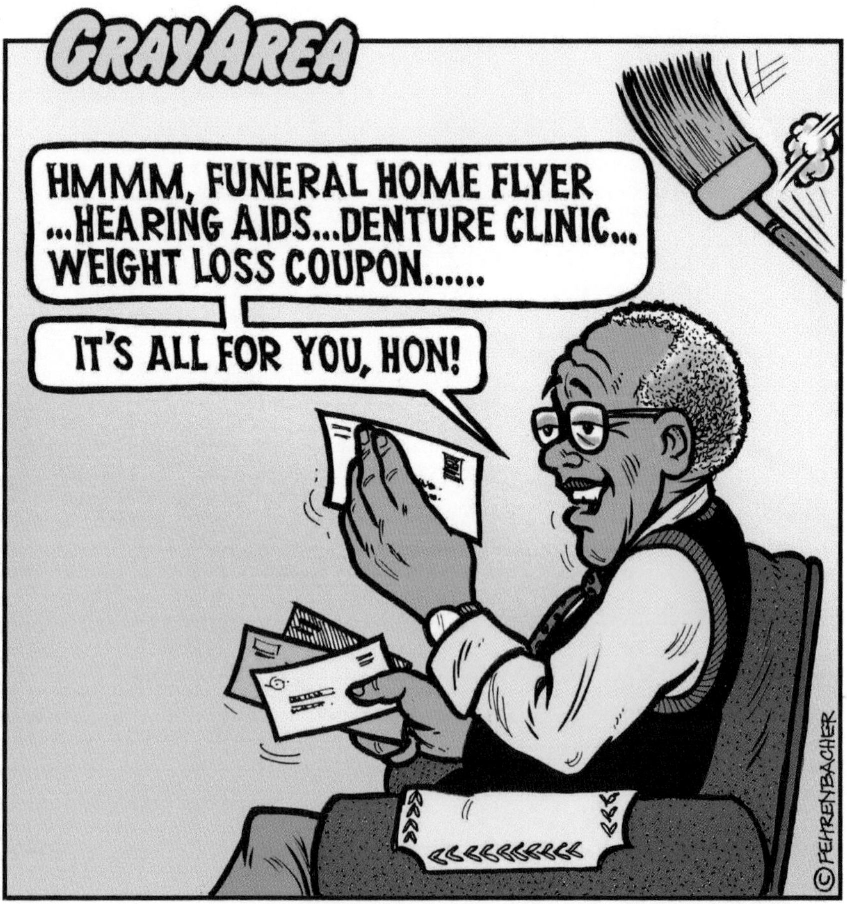
GRAYAREA
HMMM, FUNERAL HOME FLYER ...HEARING AIDS...DENTURE CLINIC... WEIGHT LOSS COUPON......
IT'S ALL FOR YOU, HON!
©FEHRENBACHER

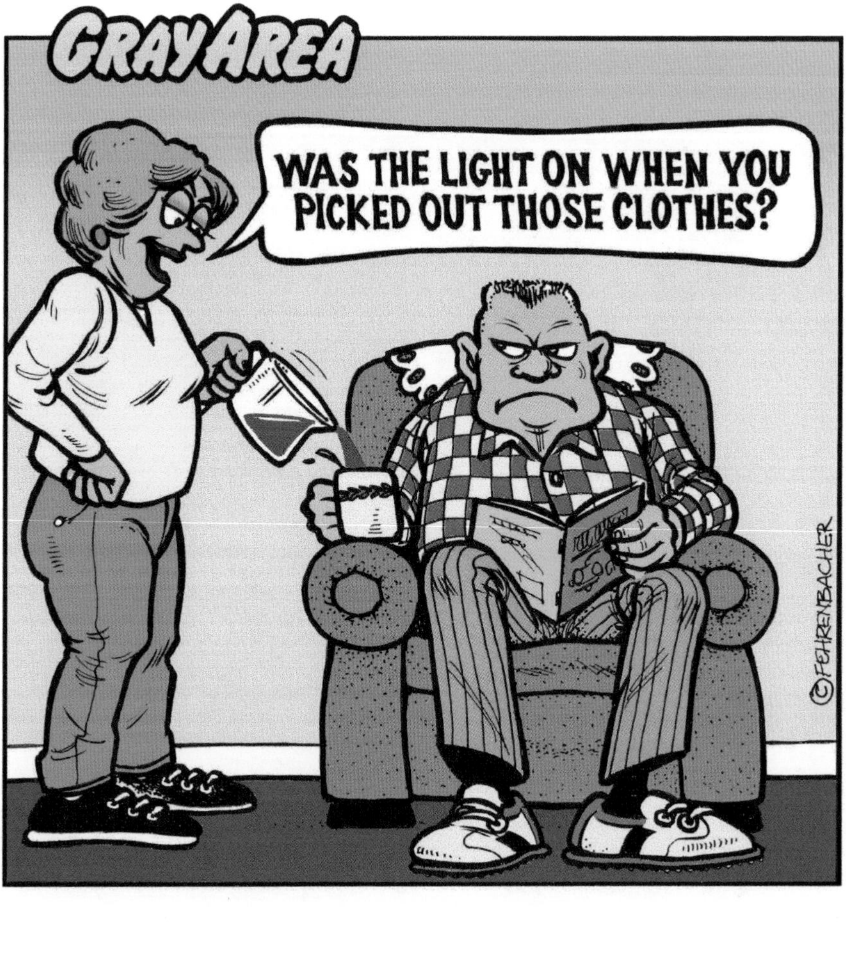
GRAY AREA
WAS THE LIGHT ON WHEN YOU PICKED OUT THOSE CLOTHES?
©FEHRENBACHER

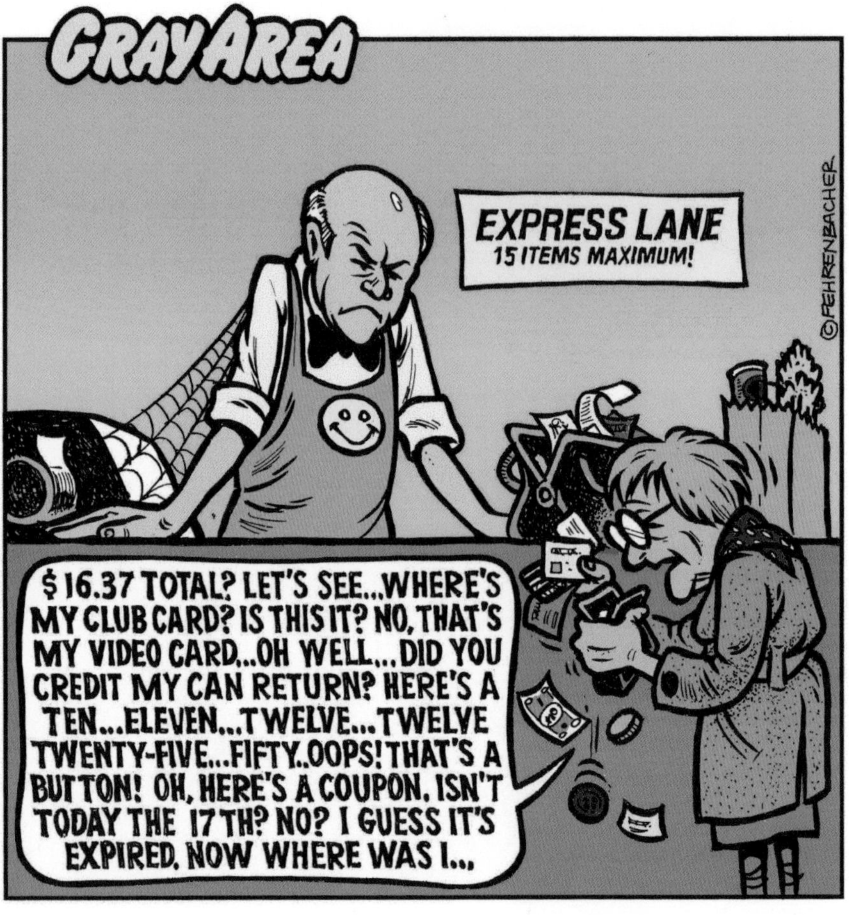
GRAY AREA
EXPRESS LANE
15 ITEMS MAXIMUM!
©FEHRENBACHER
$16.37 TOTAL? LET'S SEE...WHERE'S MY CLUB CARD? IS THIS IT? NO, THAT'S MY VIDEO CARD...OH WELL... DID YOU CREDIT MY CAN RETURN? HERE'S A TEN...ELEVEN...TWELVE...TWELVE TWENTY-FIVE...FIFTY..OOPS! THAT'S A BUTTON! OH, HERE'S A COUPON. ISN'T TODAY THE 17TH? NO? I GUESS IT'S EXPIRED. NOW WHERE WAS I...

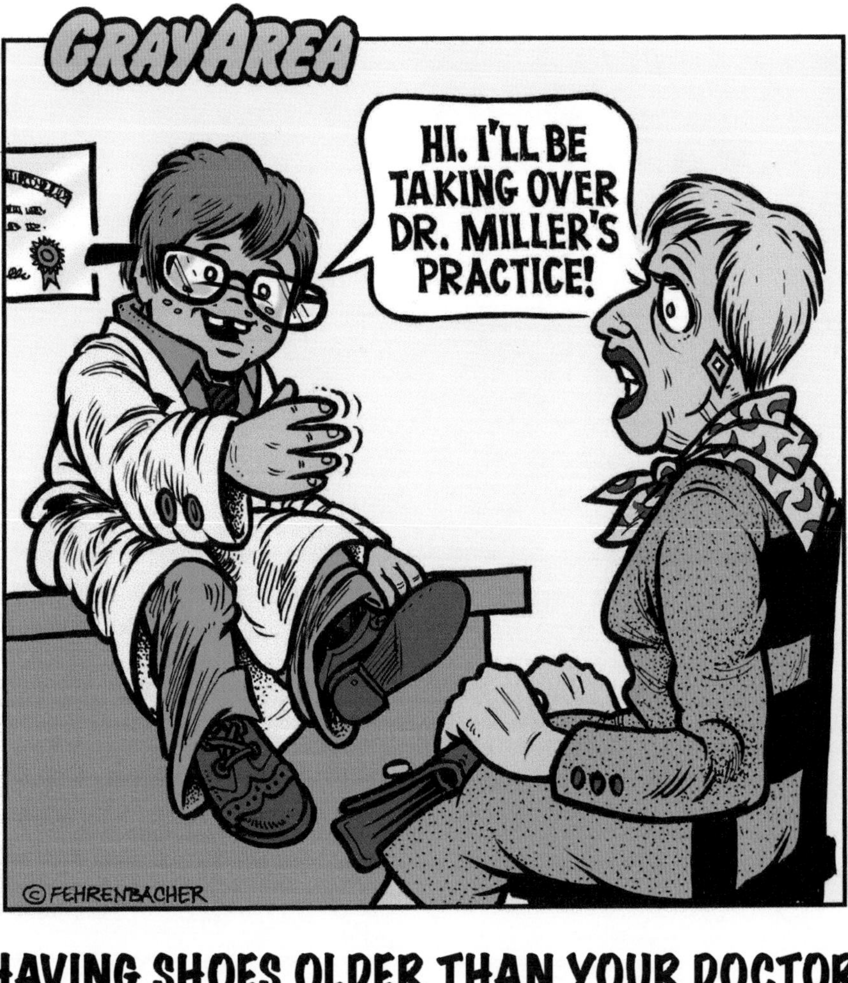
GRAY AREA
HI. I'LL BE TAKING OVER DR. MILLER'S PRACTICE!
© FEHRENBACHER

HAVING SHOES OLDER THAN YOUR DOCTOR.

GRAY AREA
I'M ROASTING!
F....FREEZING!
© FEHRENBACHER

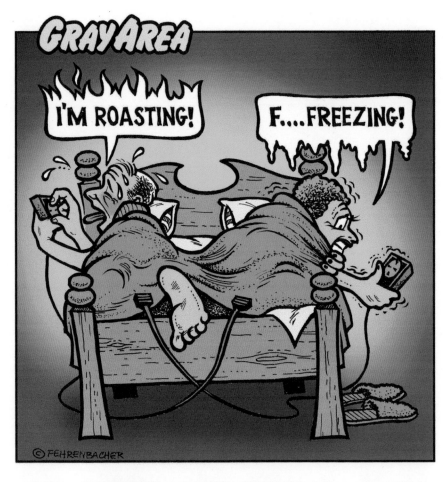

STILL TURNING EACH OTHER ON...OR OFF!

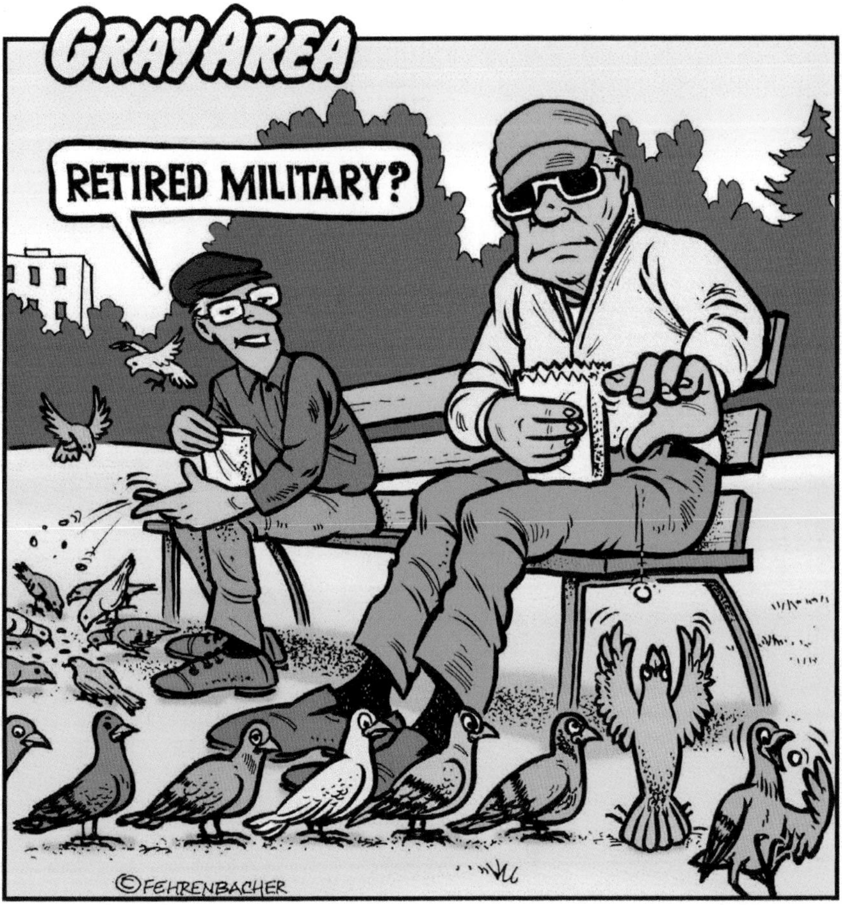
GRAYAREA
RETIRED MILITARY?
©FEHRENBACHER

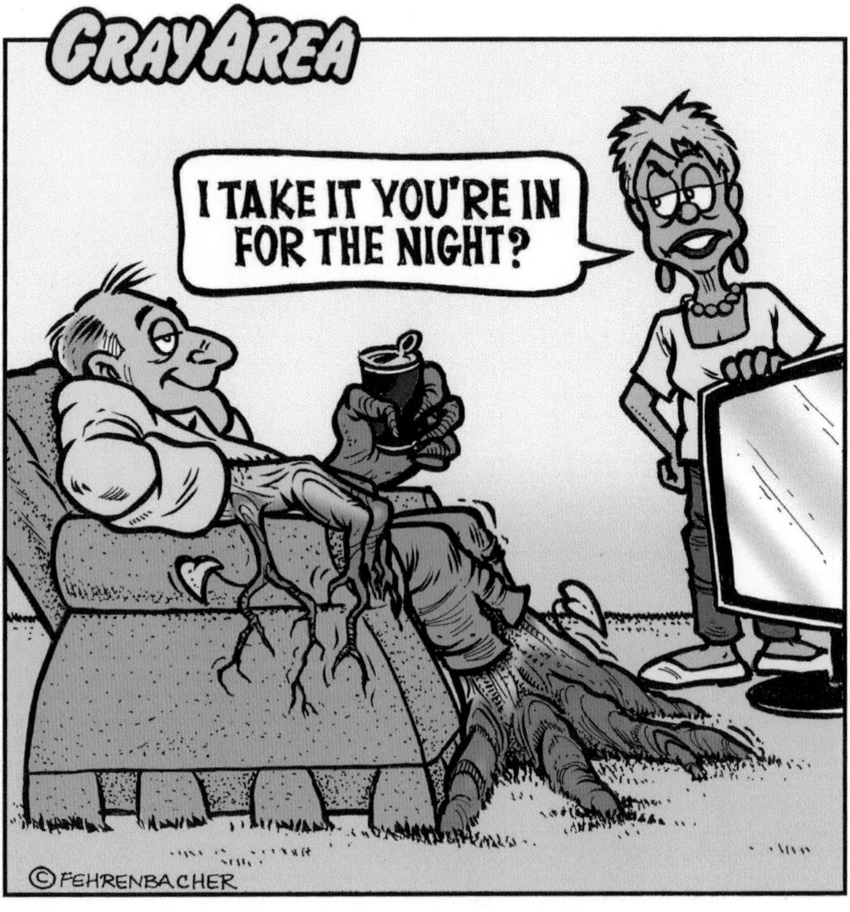
GRAY AREA
I TAKE IT YOU'RE IN FOR THE NIGHT?
© FEHRENBACHER

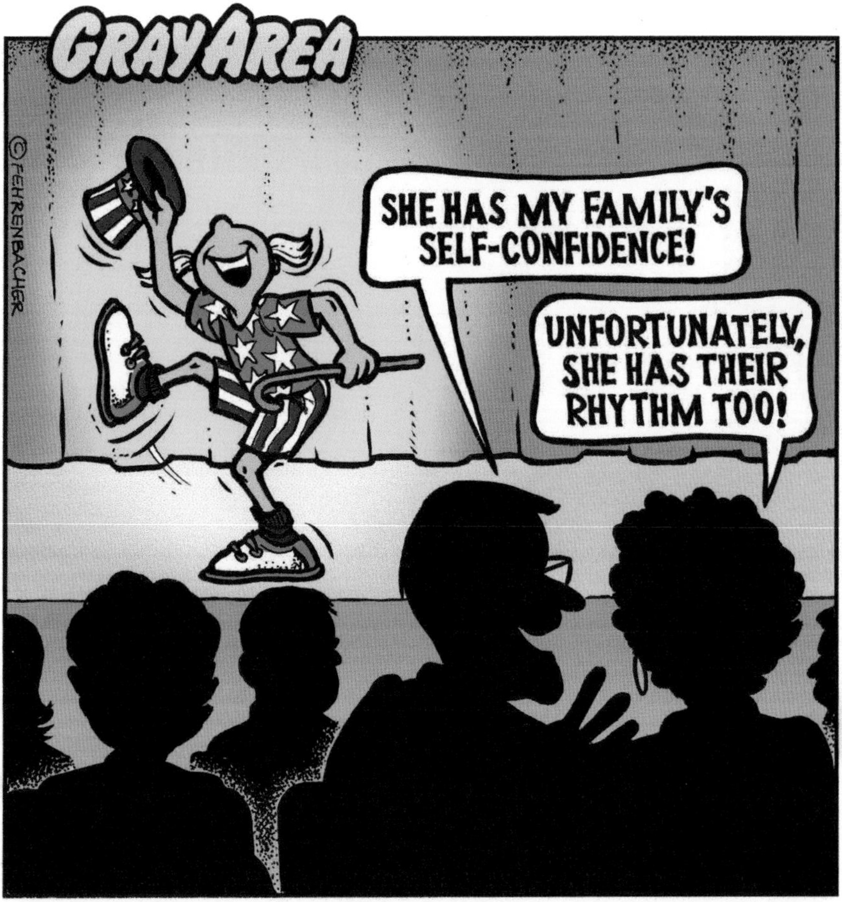
GRAY AREA
©FEHRENBACHER
SHE HAS MY FAMILY'S SELF-CONFIDENCE!
UNFORTUNATELY, SHE HAS THEIR RHYTHM TOO!

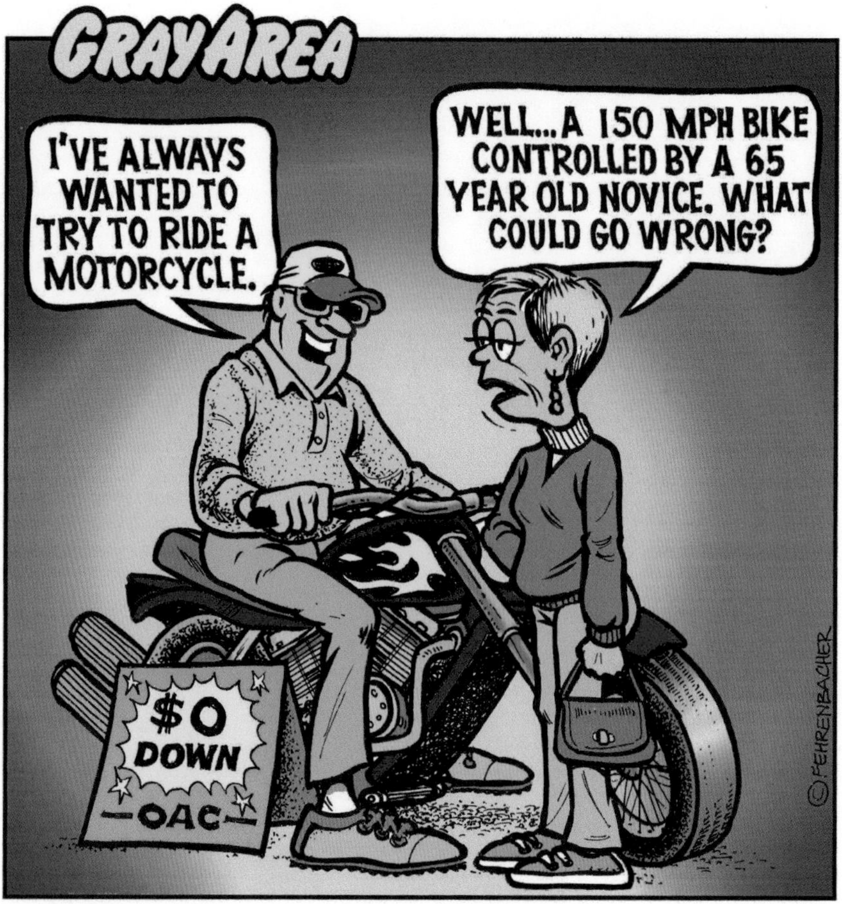
GRAY AREA
I'VE ALWAYS WANTED TO TRY TO RIDE A MOTORCYCLE.
WELL...A 150 MPH BIKE CONTROLLED BY A 65 YEAR OLD NOVICE. WHAT COULD GO WRONG?
$0 DOWN
—OAC—
©FEHRENBACHER

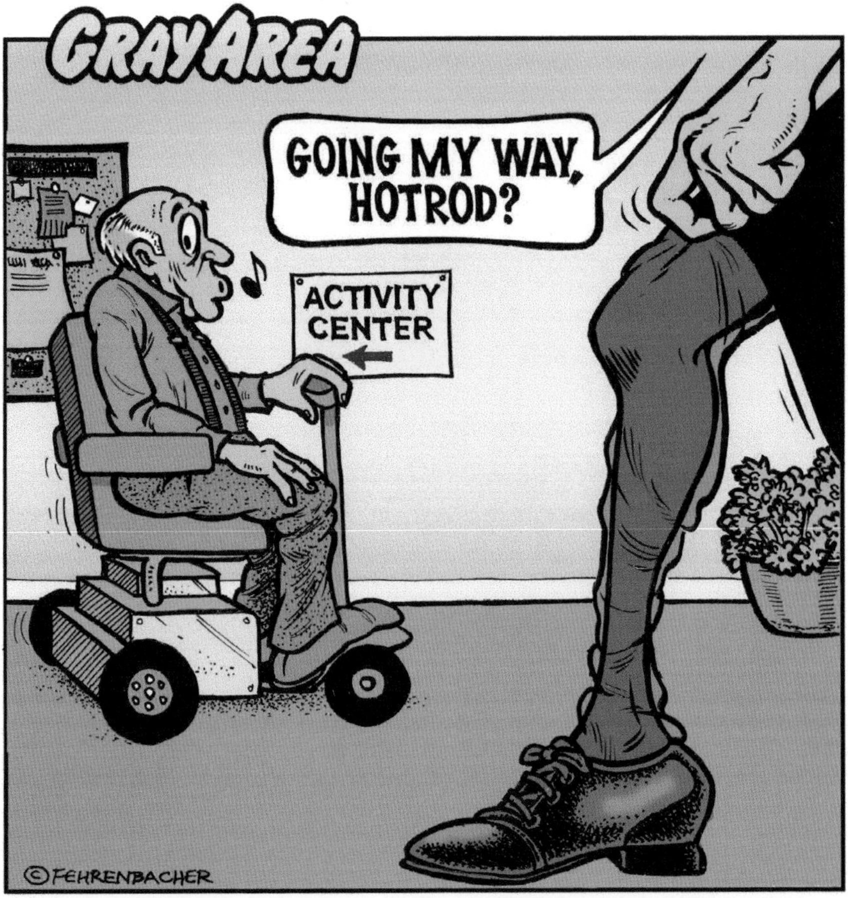
GRAY AREA
GOING MY WAY, HOTROD?
ACTIVITY CENTER
©FEHRENBACHER

FAST EDDIE PONDERS HIS NEXT MOVE!

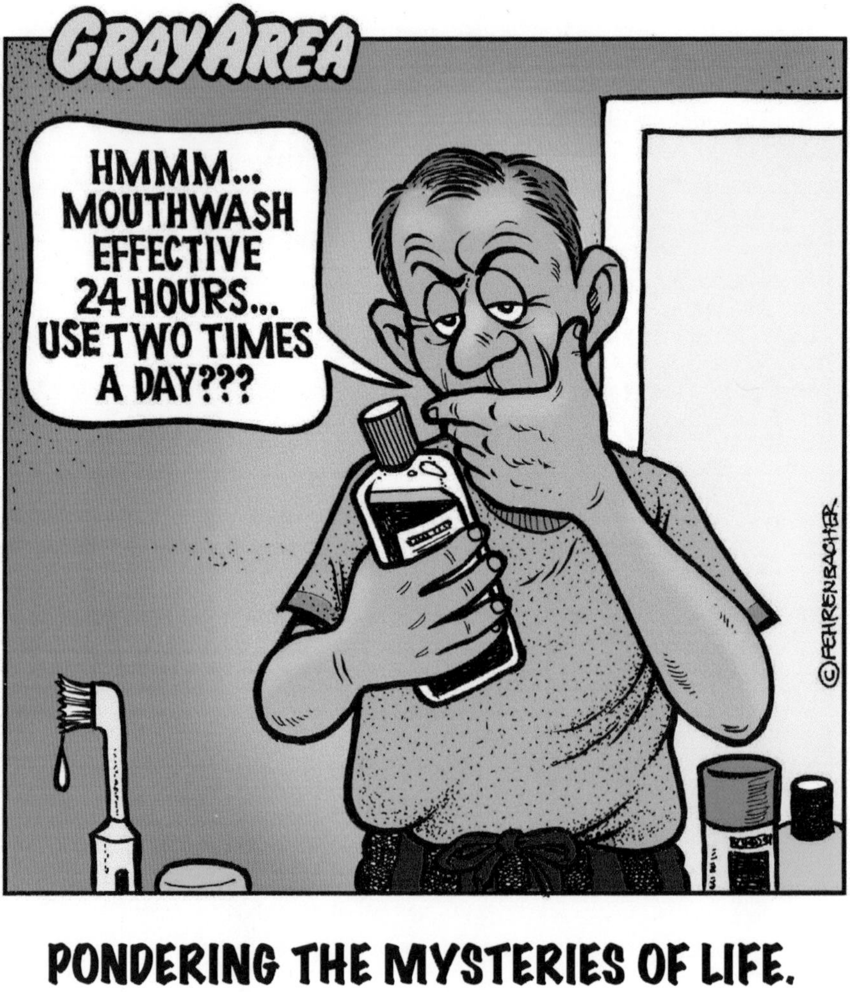
GRAY AREA
HMMM... MOUTHWASH EFFECTIVE 24 HOURS... USE TWO TIMES A DAY???
©FEHRENBACHER

PONDERING THE MYSTERIES OF LIFE.

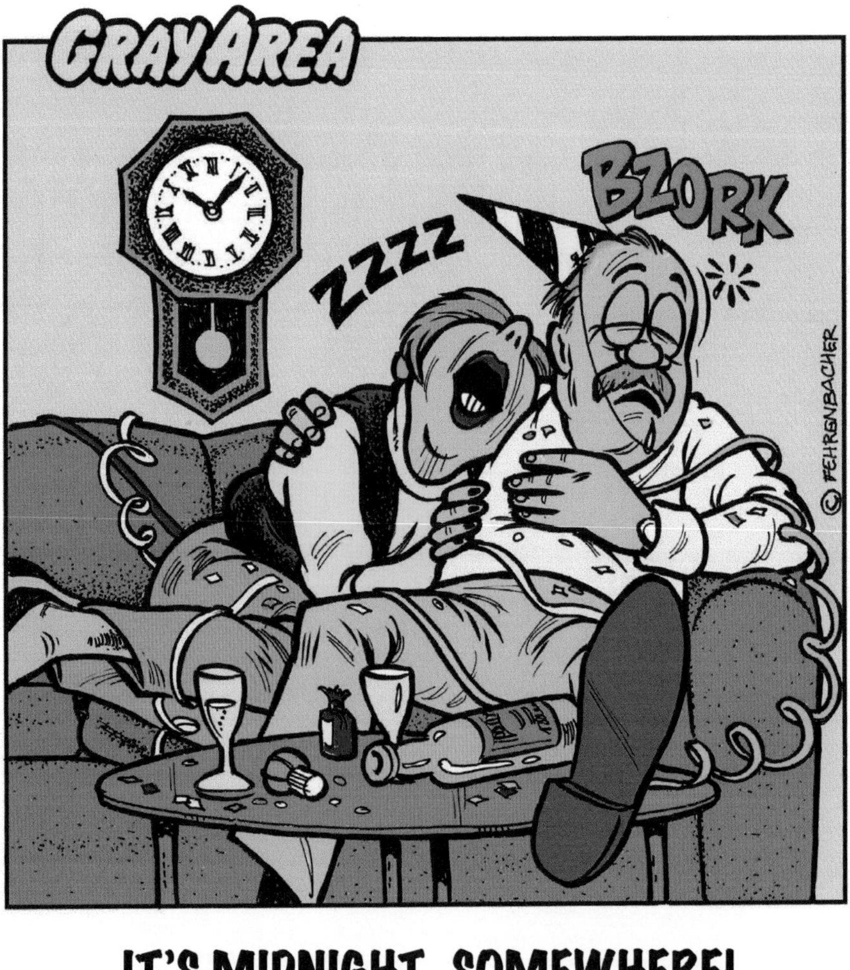
GRAY AREA
ZZZZ
BZORK
© FEHRENBACHER

IT'S MIDNIGHT...SOMEWHERE!

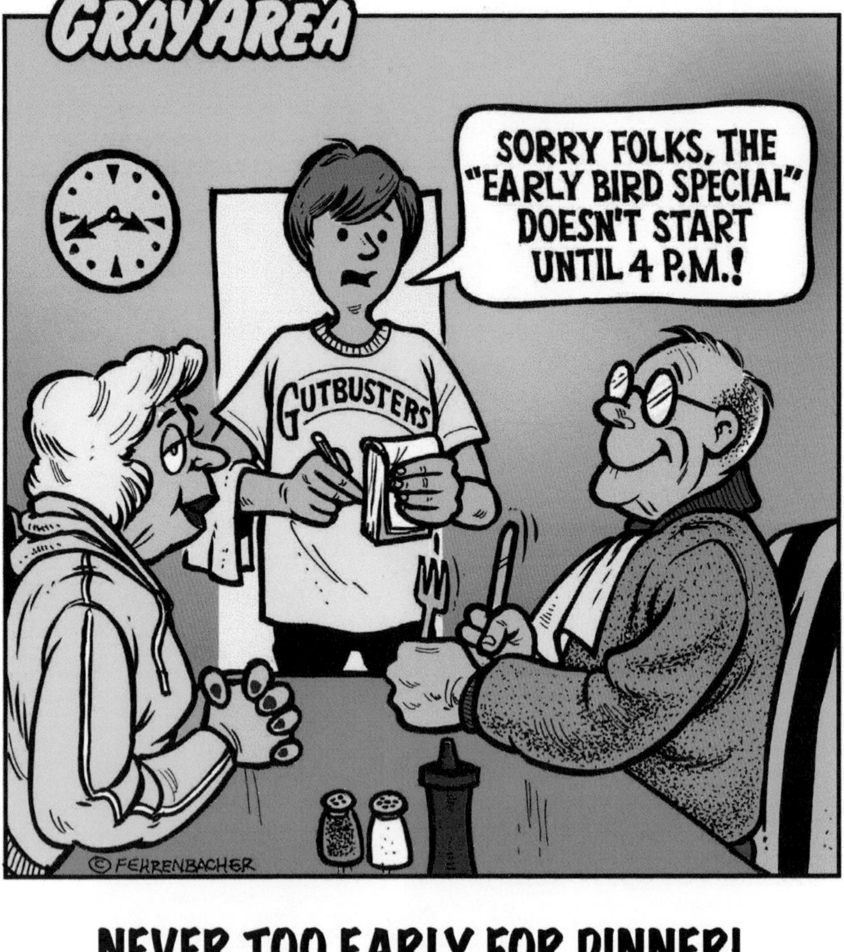
GRAYAREA
SORRY FOLKS, THE "EARLY BIRD SPECIAL" DOESN'T START UNTIL 4 P.M.!
GUTBUSTERS
© FEHRENBACHER

NEVER TOO EARLY FOR DINNER!

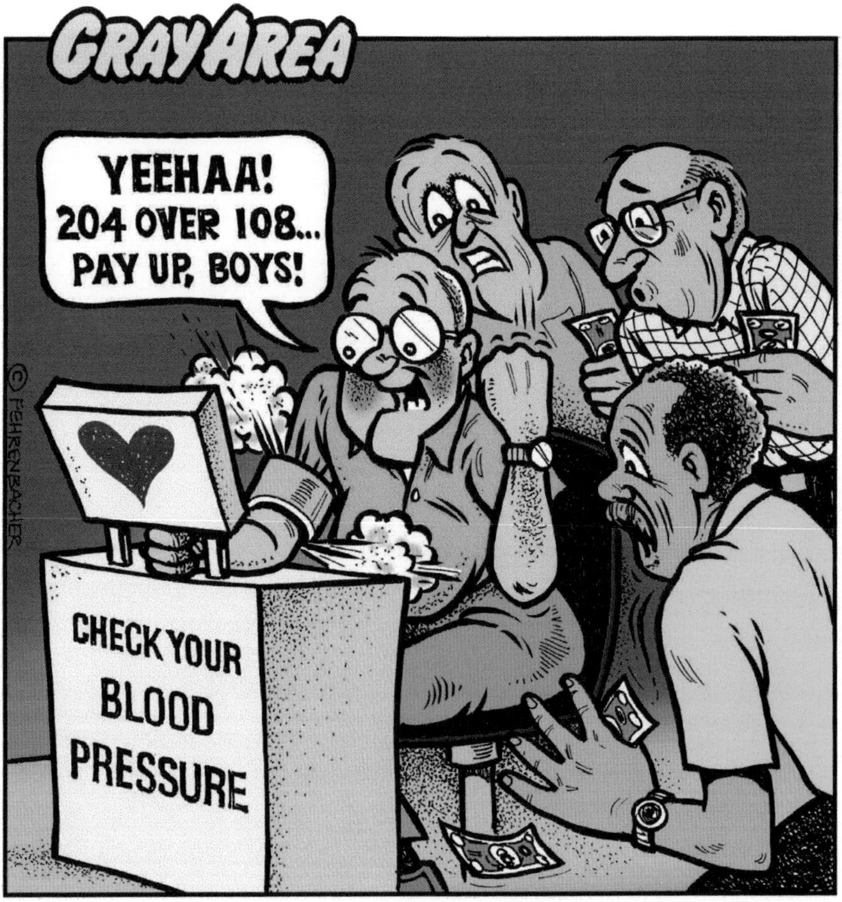
GRAY AREA
YEEHAA! 204 OVER 108... PAY UP, BOYS!
CHECK YOUR BLOOD PRESSURE
© FEHRENBACHER

AL TAKES THE HIGHLY COMPETITIVE WEEKLY BP POOL WITH A PERSONAL HIGH!

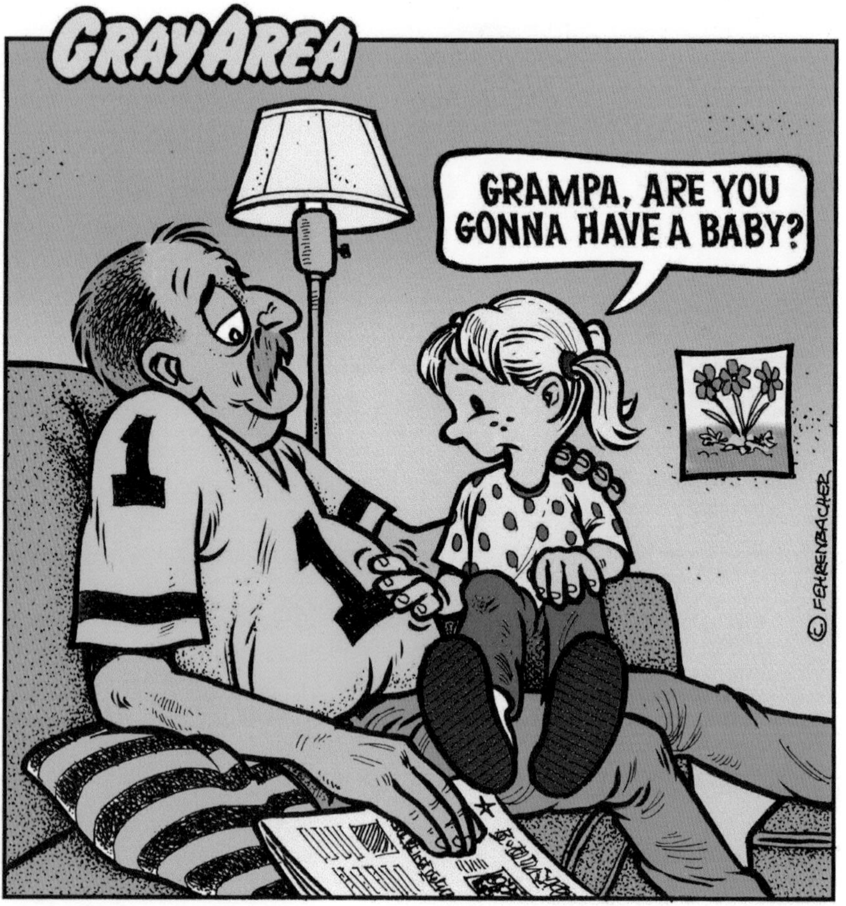
GRAY AREA
GRAMPA, ARE YOU GONNA HAVE A BABY?
© FEHRENBACHER

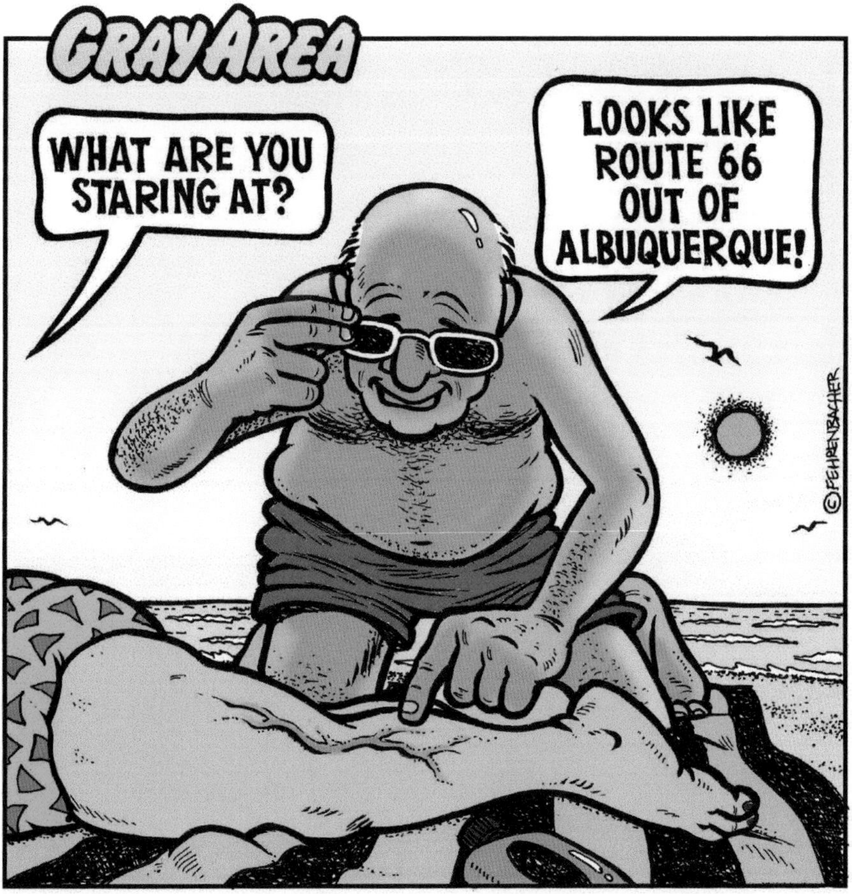
GRAY AREA
WHAT ARE YOU STARING AT?
LOOKS LIKE ROUTE 66 OUT OF ALBUQUERQUE!
©FEHRENBACHER

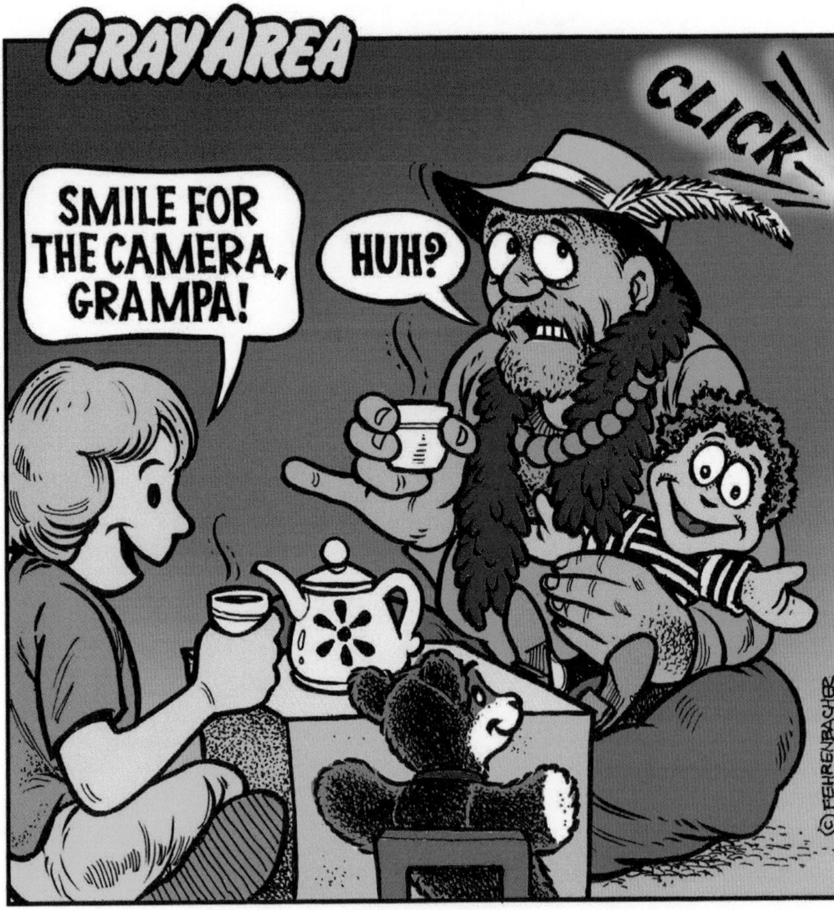
GRAY AREA
CLICK
SMILE FOR THE CAMERA, GRAMPA!
HUH?
© FEHRENBACHER

BIG RON SOON BECOMES A FACEBOOK HIT!

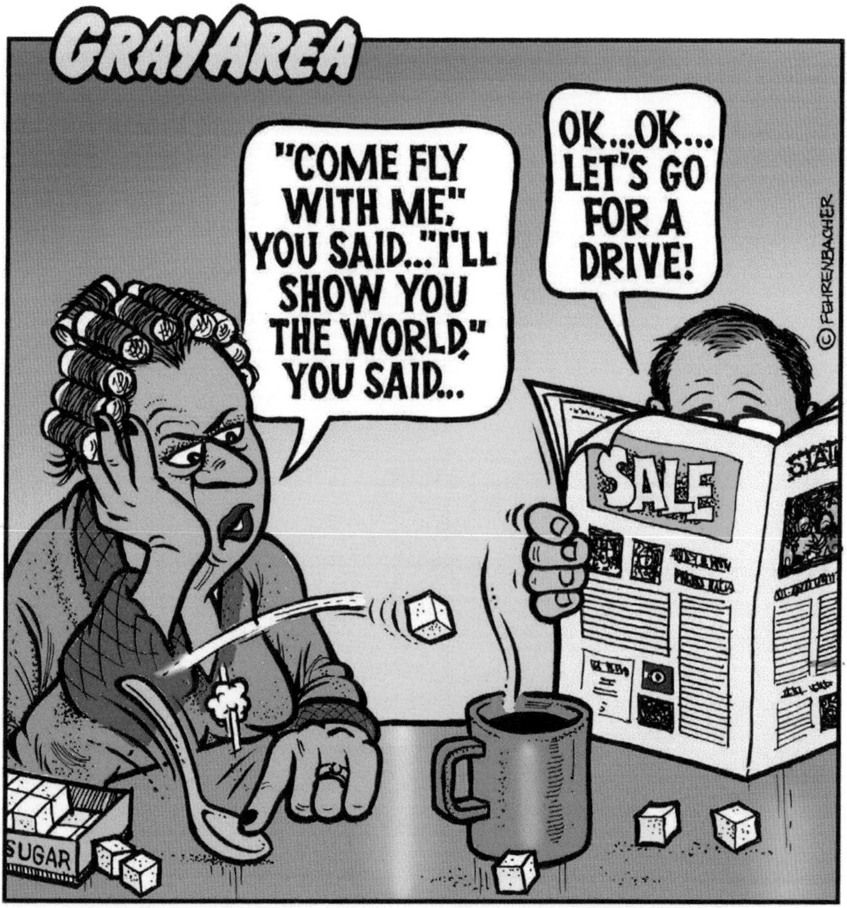
GRAY AREA
"COME FLY WITH ME," YOU SAID..."I'LL SHOW YOU THE WORLD," YOU SAID...
OK...OK... LET'S GO FOR A DRIVE!
SALE
SUGAR
© FEHRENBACHER

HONORING YOUR COMMITMENTS.

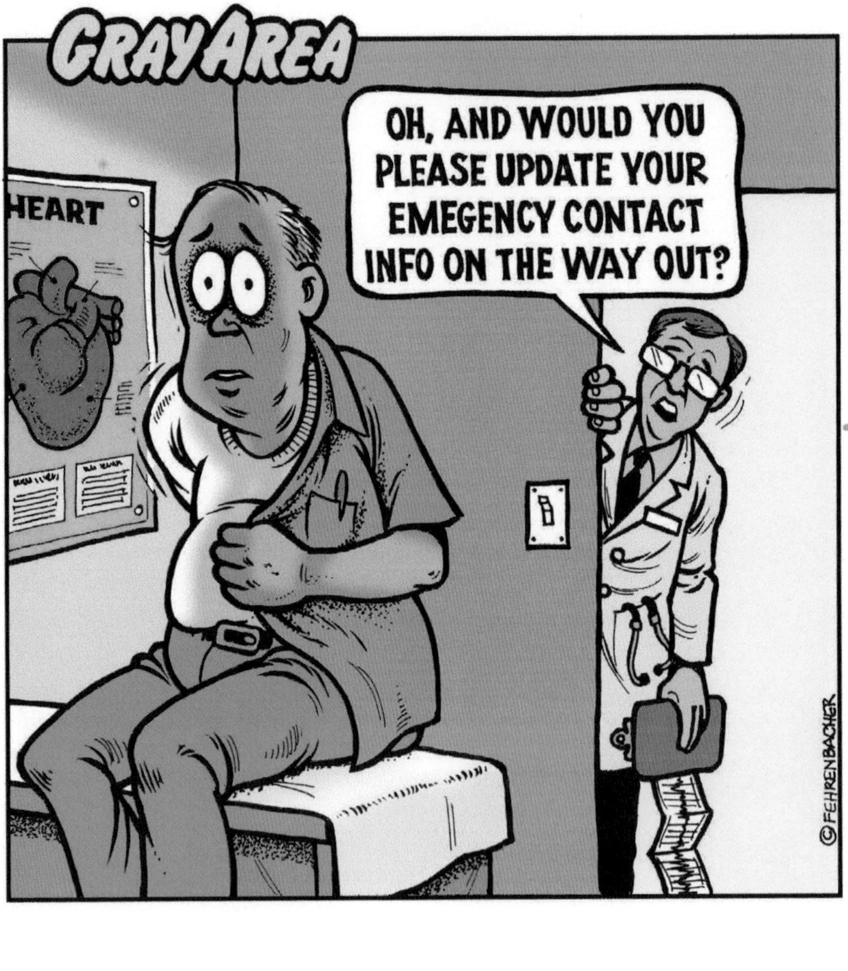
GRAY AREA
HEART
OH, AND WOULD YOU PLEASE UPDATE YOUR EMEGENCY CONTACT INFO ON THE WAY OUT?
©FEHRENBACHER

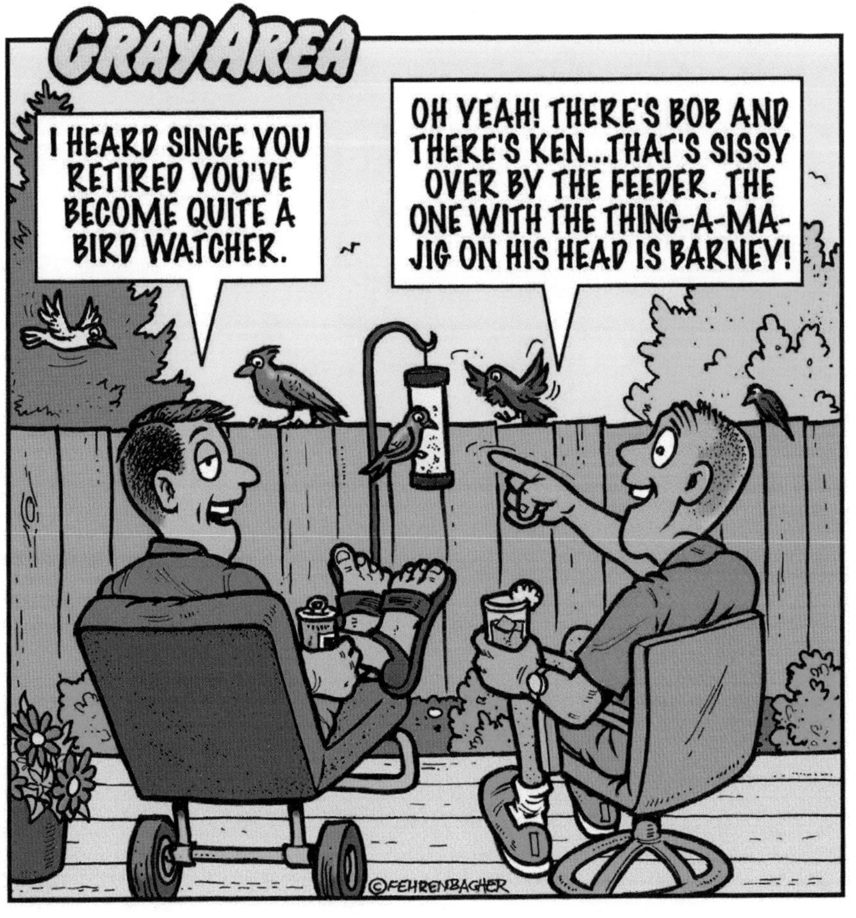
GRAY AREA
I HEARD SINCE YOU RETIRED YOU'VE BECOME QUITE A BIRD WATCHER.
OH YEAH! THERE'S BOB AND THERE'S KEN...THAT'S SISSY OVER BY THE FEEDER. THE ONE WITH THE THING-A-MA-JIG ON HIS HEAD IS BARNEY!
©FEHRENBACHER

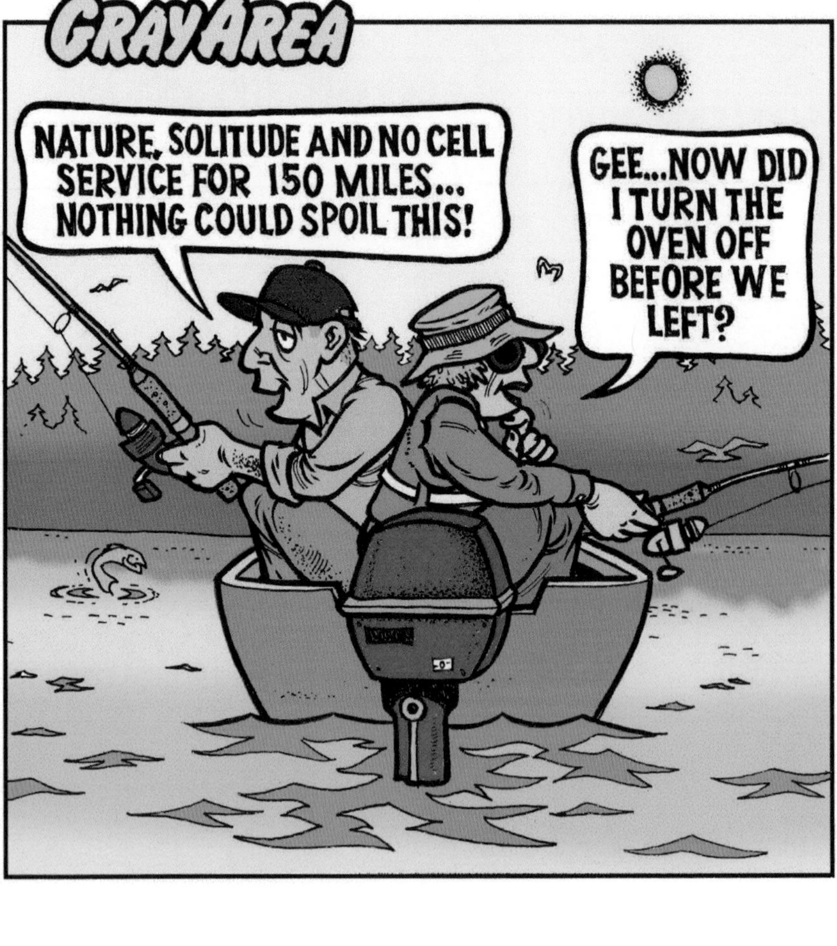
GRAY AREA
NATURE, SOLITUDE AND NO CELL SERVICE FOR 150 MILES... NOTHING COULD SPOIL THIS!
GEE...NOW DID I TURN THE OVEN OFF BEFORE WE LEFT?

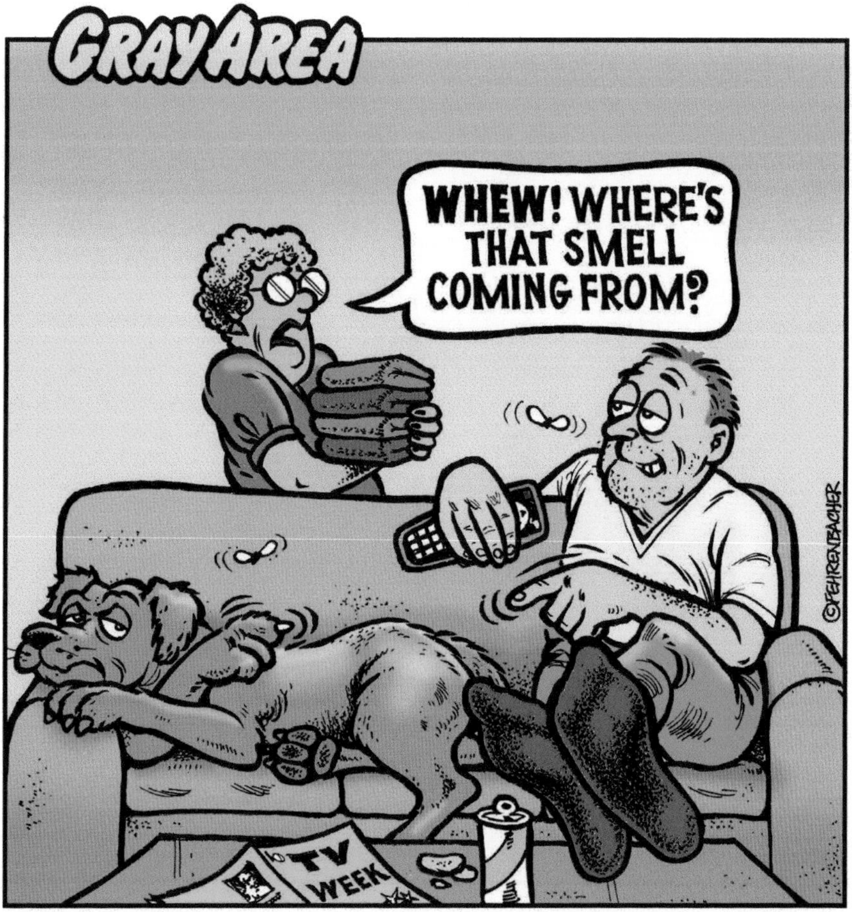
GRAY AREA
WHEW! WHERE'S THAT SMELL COMING FROM?
TV WEEK
©FEHRENBACHER

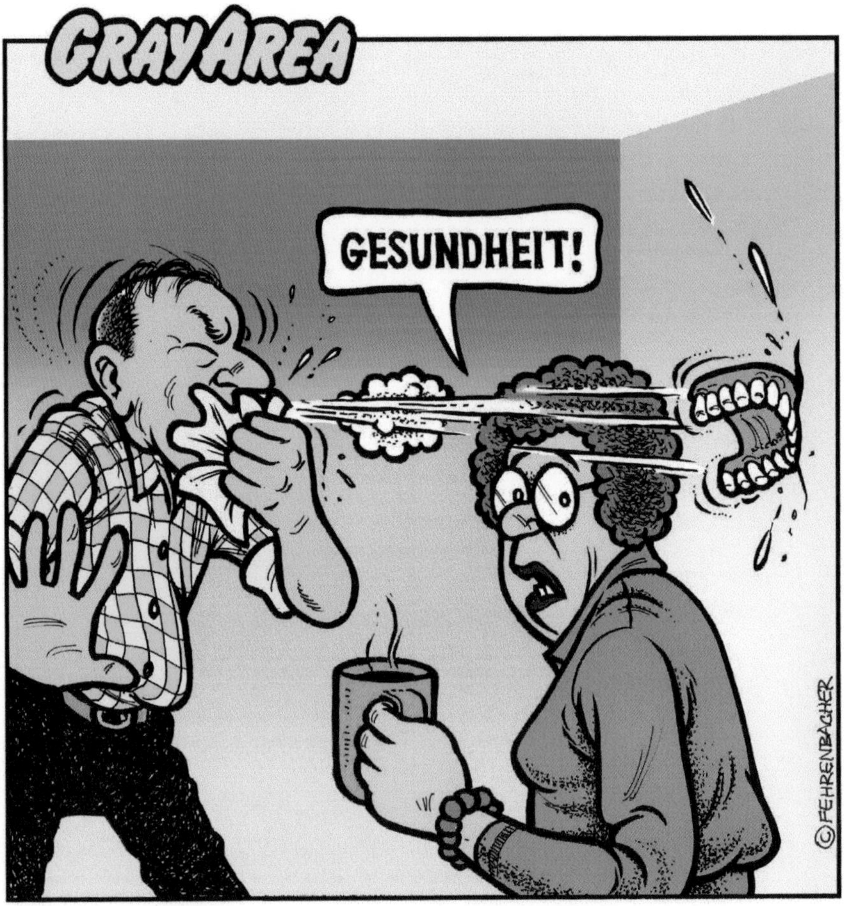
GRAYAREA
GESUNDHEIT!
©FEHRENBACHER

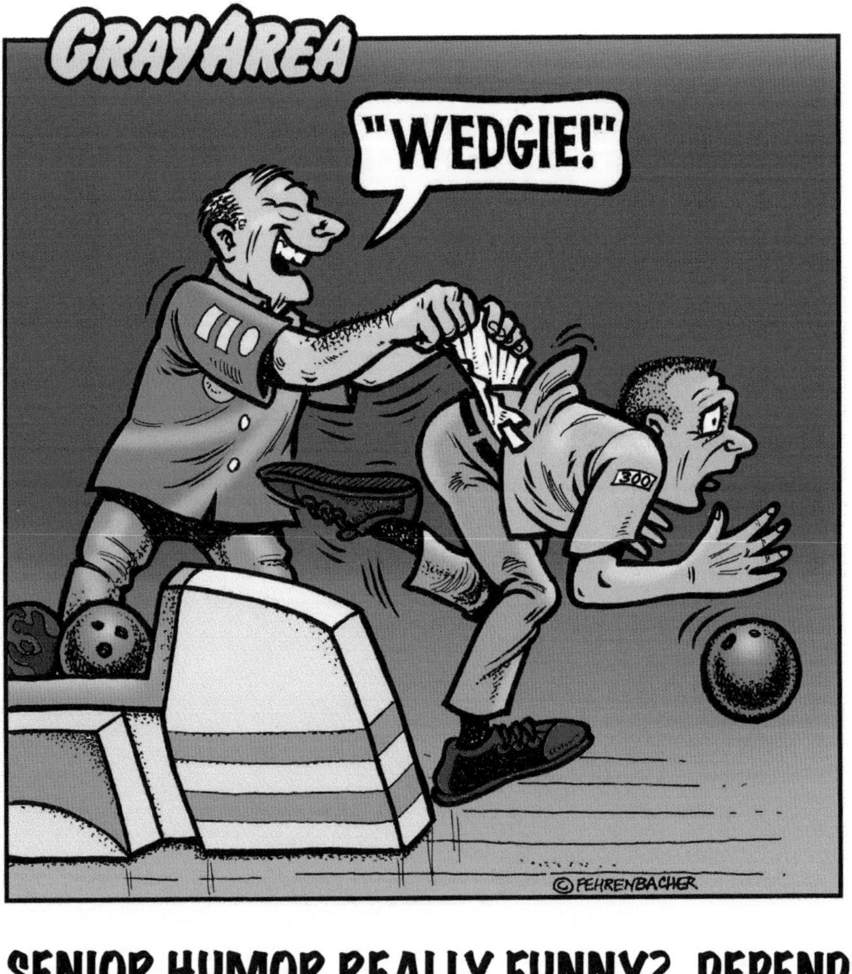
GRAYAREA
"WEDGIE!"
300
©FEHRENBACHER

IS SENIOR HUMOR REALLY FUNNY?...DEPENDS!

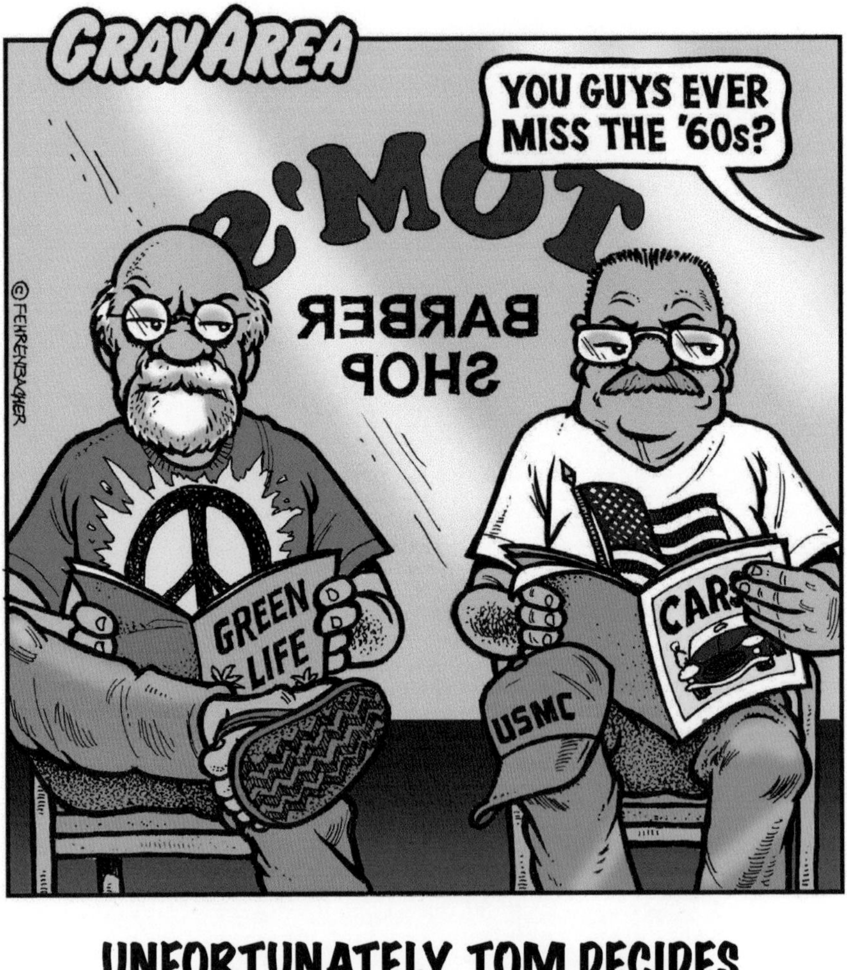
GRAY AREA
YOU GUYS EVER MISS THE '60s?
TOM'S
BARBER SHOP
© FEHRENBACHER
GREEN LIFE
CARS
USMC

UNFORTUNATELY, TOM DECIDES TO INITIATE A DISCUSSION!

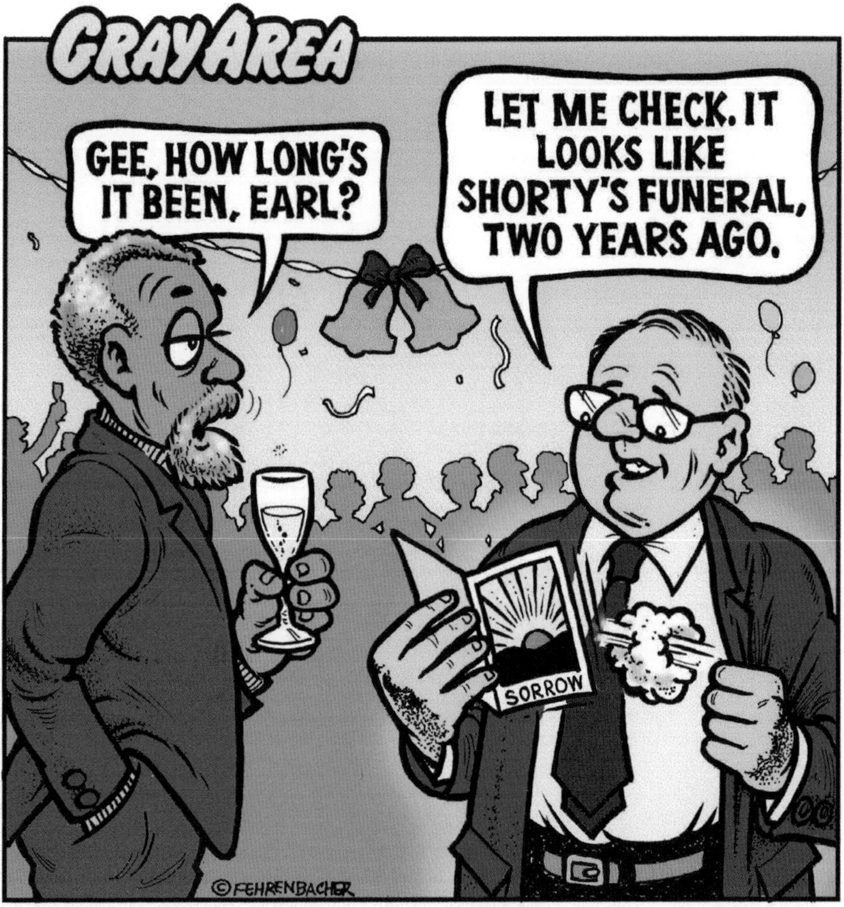
GRAY AREA
GEE, HOW LONG'S IT BEEN, EARL?
LET ME CHECK. IT LOOKS LIKE SHORTY'S FUNERAL, TWO YEARS AGO.
SORROW
©FEHRENBACHER

THE ALL-PURPOSE DARK BLAZER FOR SENIORS.

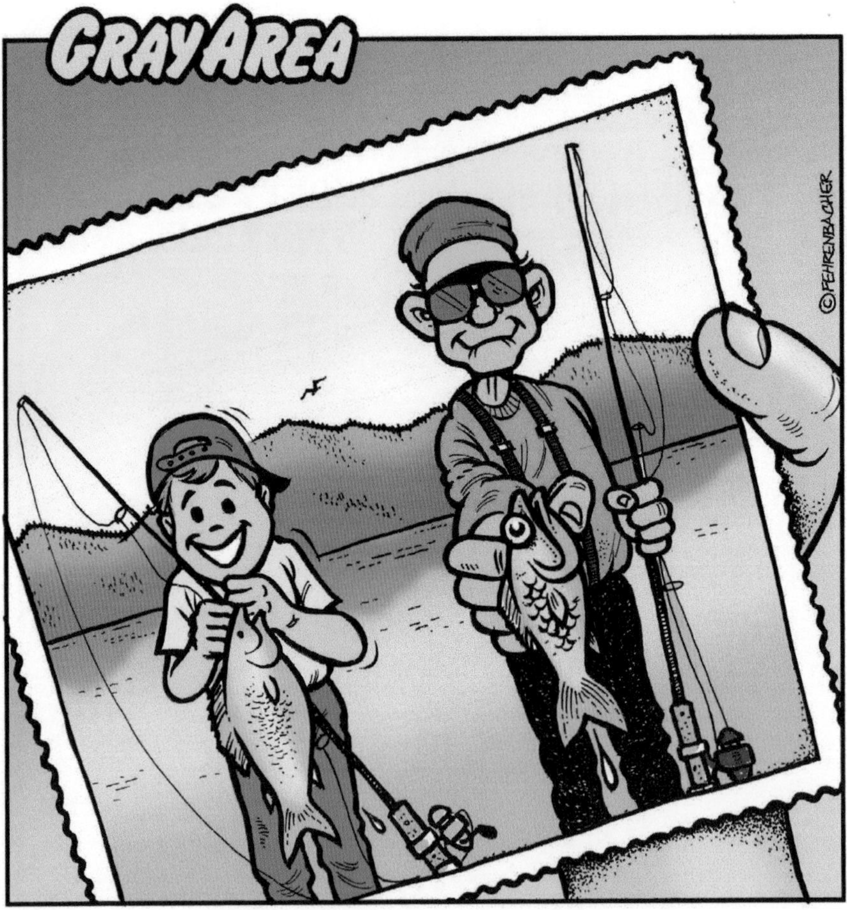
GRAY AREA
©FEHRENBACHER

"HEY GRAMPA...IN THE PHOTO, HOW COME YOUR FISH LOOKS AS BIG AS MINE?"

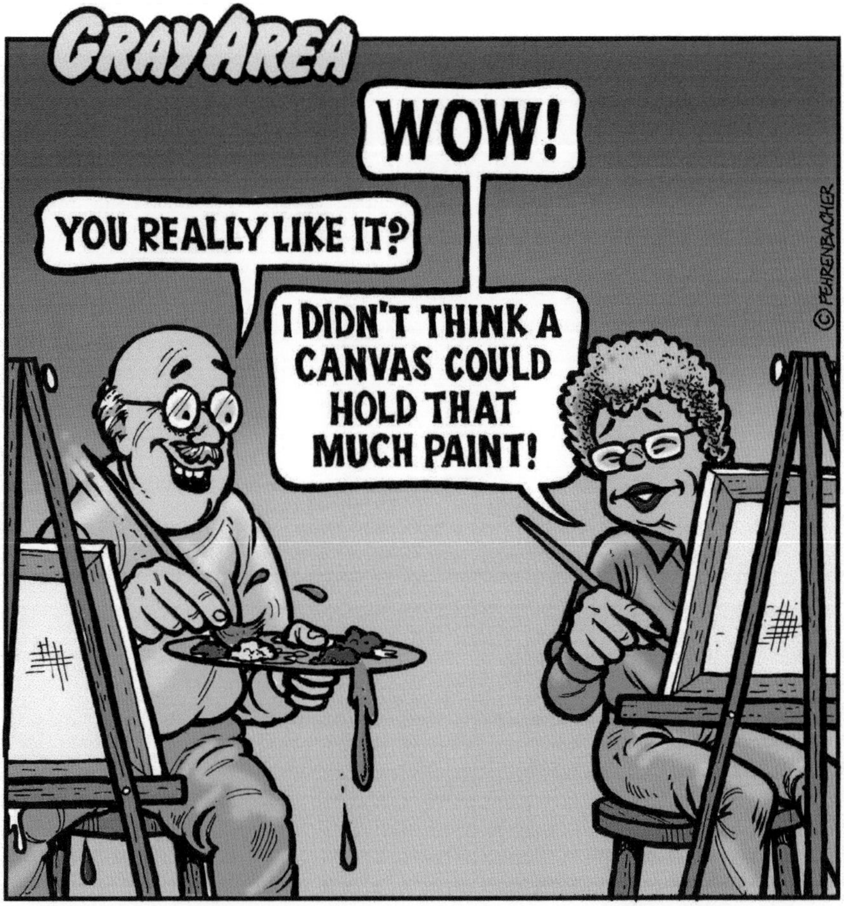
GRAY AREA
WOW!
YOU REALLY LIKE IT?
I DIDN'T THINK A CANVAS COULD HOLD THAT MUCH PAINT!
© FEHRENBACHER

MASTERING NEW FIELDS OF INTEREST.

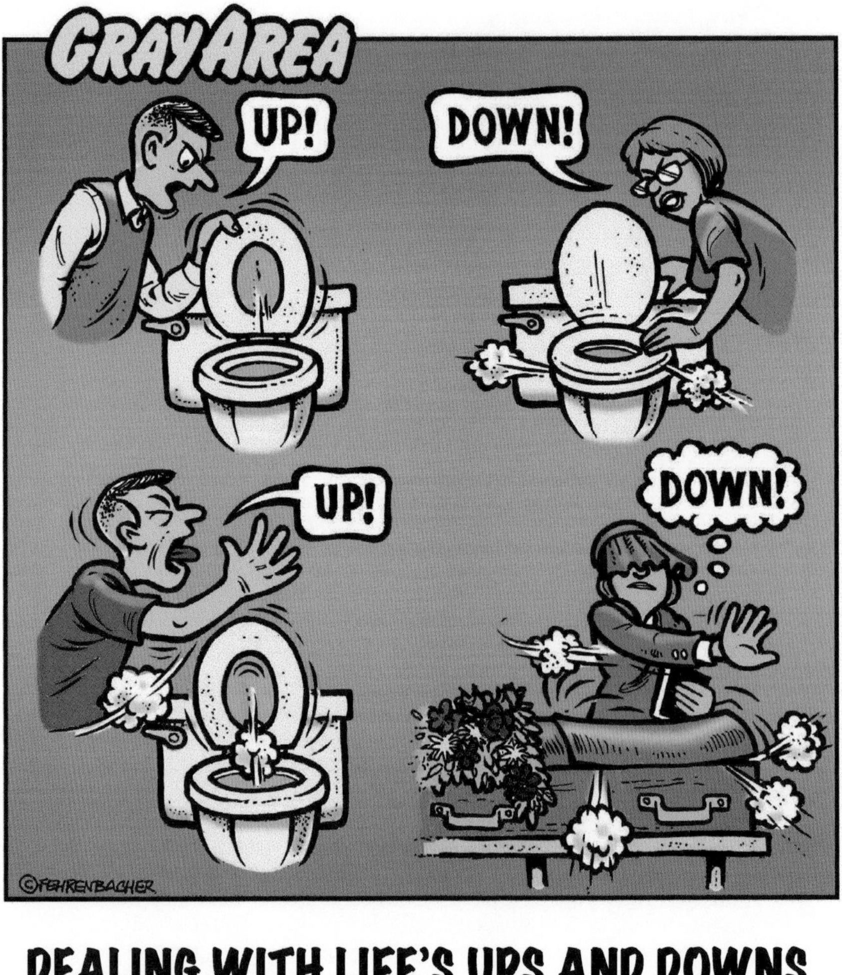
GRAY AREA
UP!
DOWN!
UP!
DOWN!
©FEHRENBACHER

DEALING WITH LIFE'S UPS AND DOWNS.

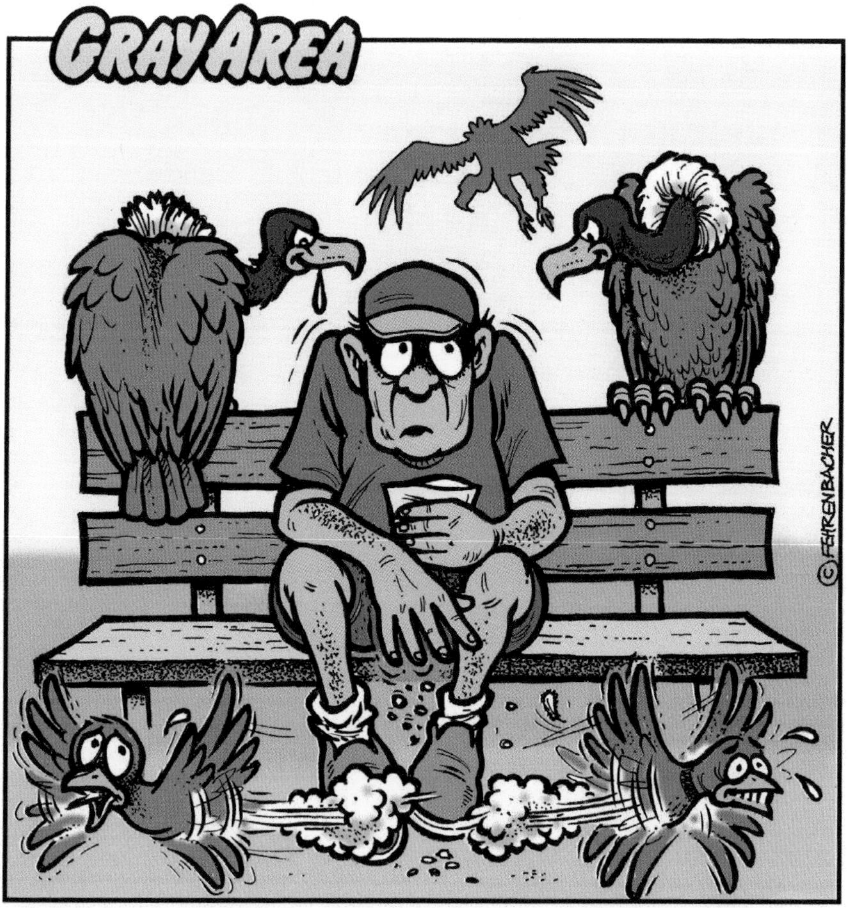
GRAY AREA
© FEHRENBACHER

FRED SUDDENLY REALIZES THAT FEEDING THE BIRDS HAS TAKEN AN IRONIC TWIST!

GRAY AREA
I THINK HE NEEDS MOUTH-TO -MOUTH.
YOU KNOW HIM BETTER THAN I DO!
YOU CALLING 9-1-1, JERRY?
NO, I'M CALLING JOSE, WE'LL NEED ANOTHER PLAYER.
ACK... ACK...
IT'LL BE OUR BALL WHEN THIS IS OVER!

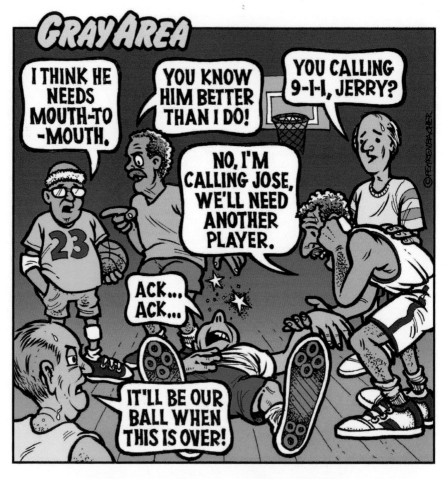

THE CAMARADERIE AND COMPASSION OF PLAYING "GEEZER BALL."

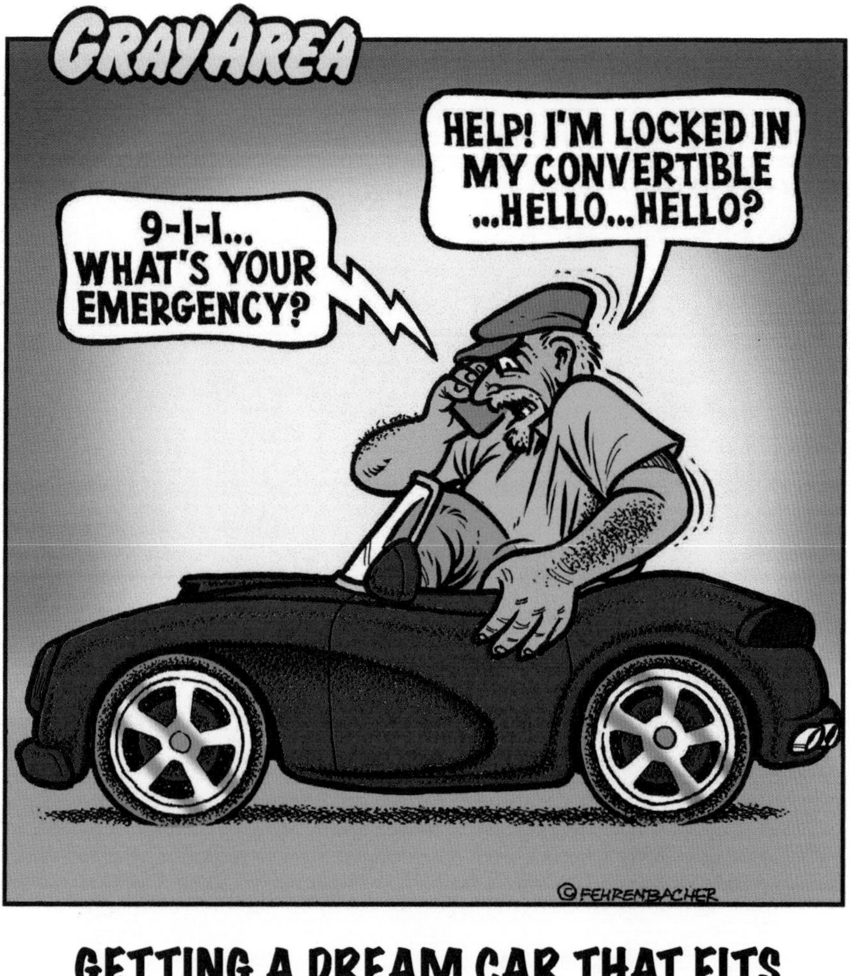
GRAY AREA
9-1-1...
WHAT'S YOUR
EMERGENCY?
HELP! I'M LOCKED IN
MY CONVERTIBLE
...HELLO...HELLO?
© FEHRENBACHER

GETTING A DREAM CAR THAT FITS
YOUR BILLFOLD, BUT NOT YOUR BUTT!

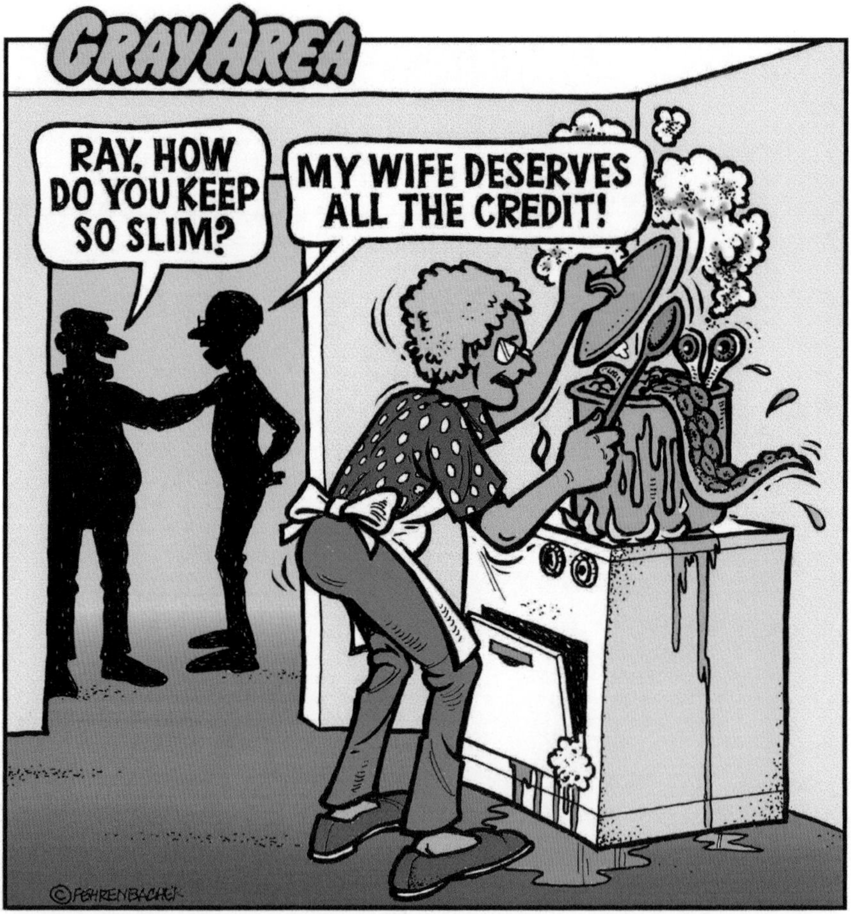
GRAY AREA
RAY, HOW DO YOU KEEP SO SLIM?
MY WIFE DESERVES ALL THE CREDIT!
©FEHRENBACHER

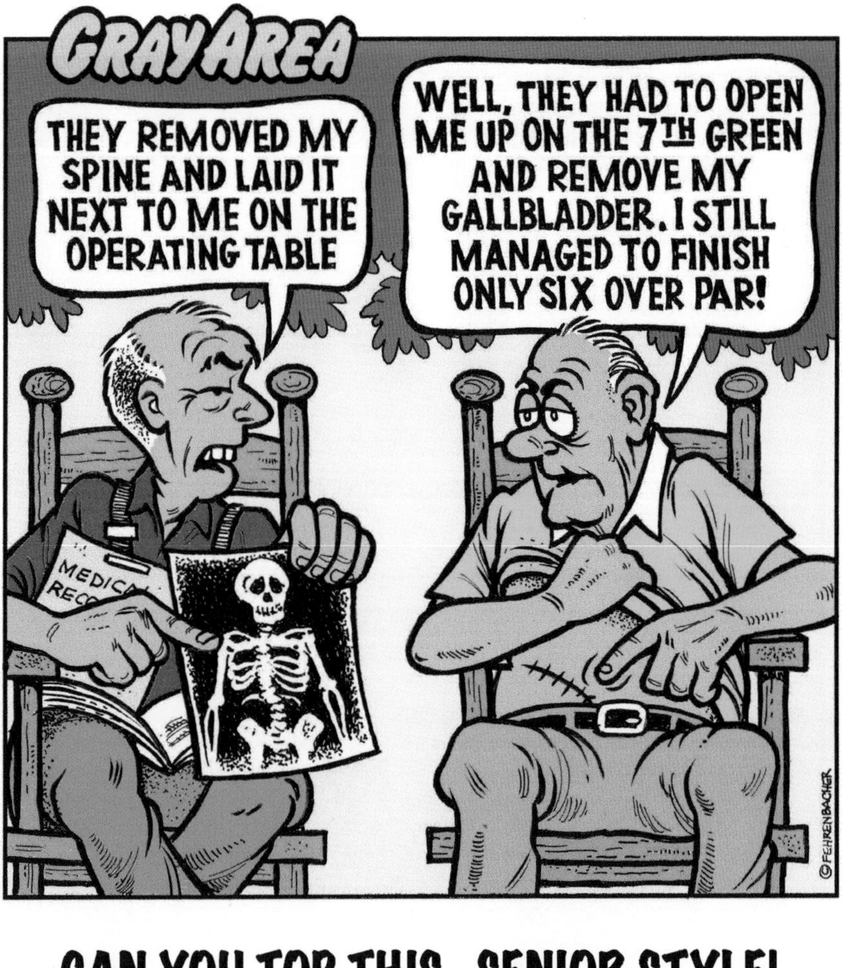
GRAY AREA
THEY REMOVED MY SPINE AND LAID IT NEXT TO ME ON THE OPERATING TABLE
WELL, THEY HAD TO OPEN ME UP ON THE 7TH GREEN AND REMOVE MY GALLBLADDER. I STILL MANAGED TO FINISH ONLY SIX OVER PAR!
©FEHRENBACHER

CAN YOU TOP THIS...SENIOR STYLE!

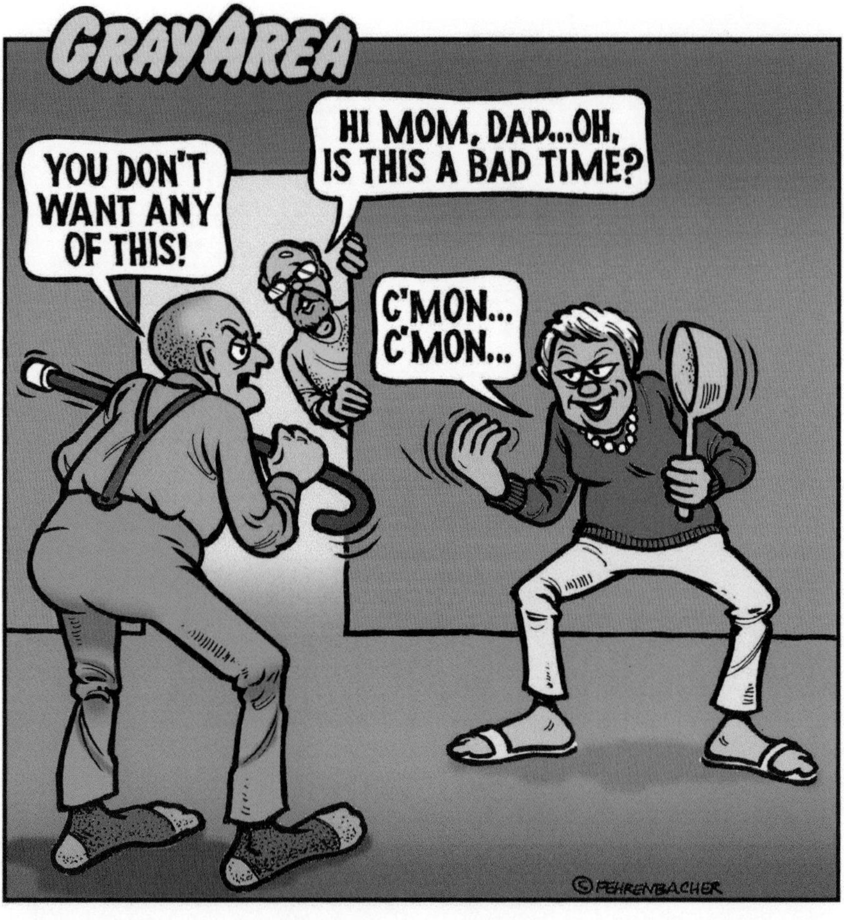
GRAY AREA
YOU DON'T WANT ANY OF THIS!
HI MOM, DAD...OH, IS THIS A BAD TIME?
C'MON... C'MON...
©FEHRENBACHER

SENIORS STILL HAVE THEIR LITTLE SPATS.

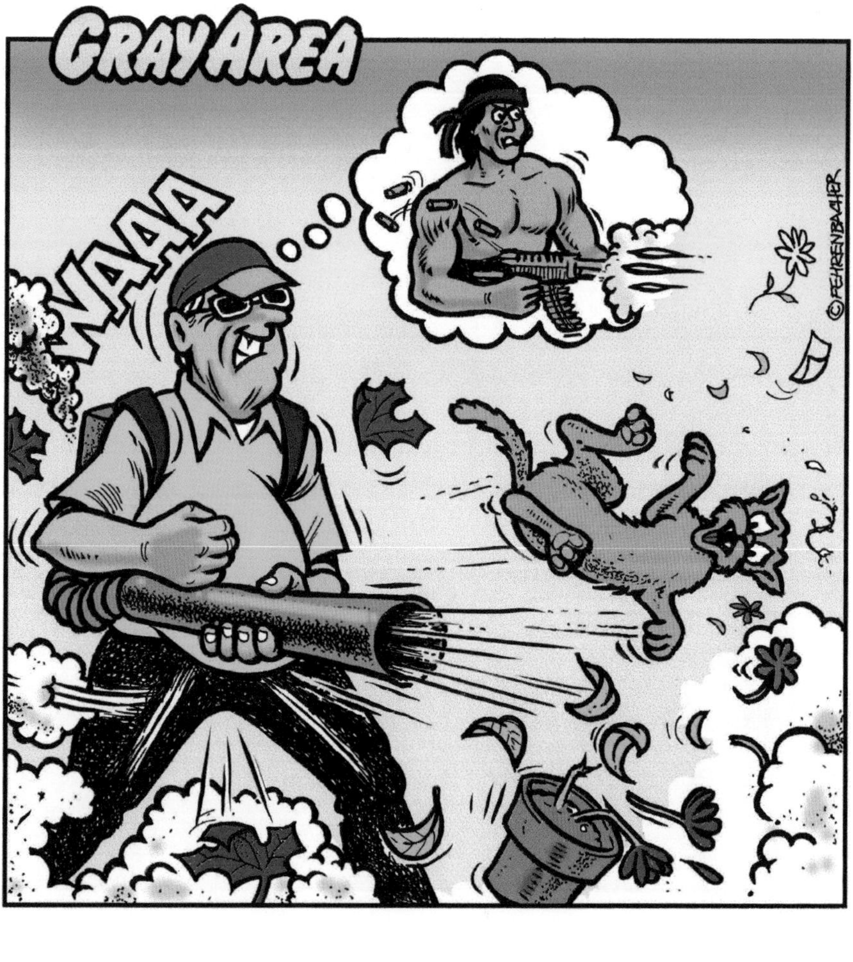
GRAY AREA
WAAA
©FEHRENBACHER

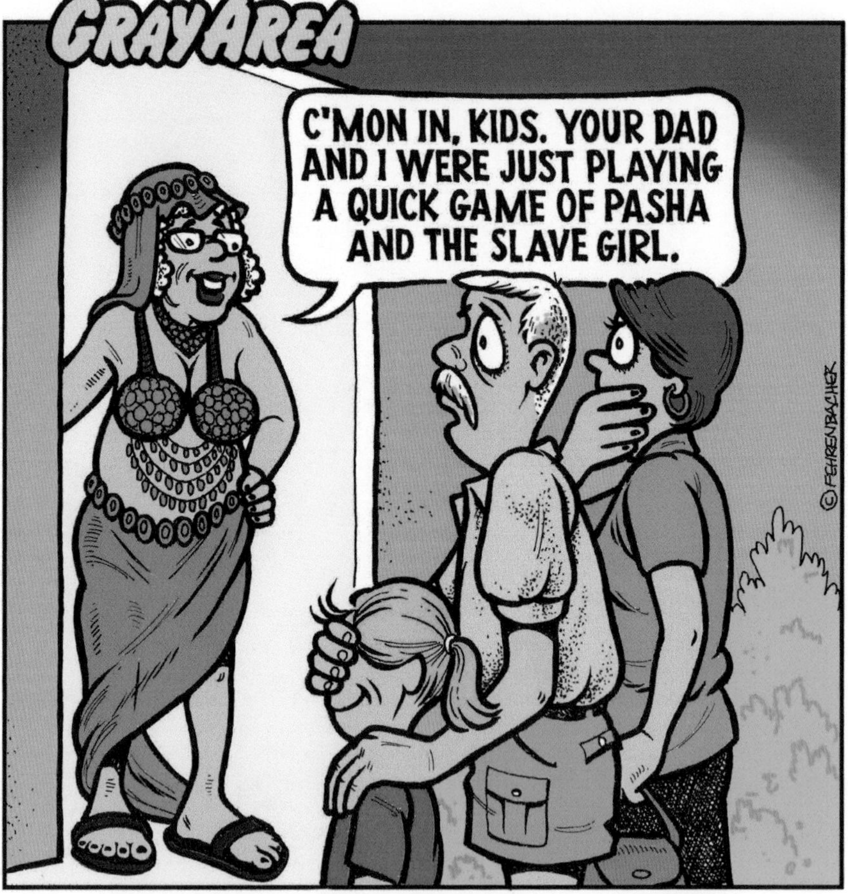
GRAY AREA
C'MON IN, KIDS. YOUR DAD AND I WERE JUST PLAYING A QUICK GAME OF PASHA AND THE SLAVE GIRL.
© FEHRENBACHER

KEEPING THE "MAGIC" ALIVE.

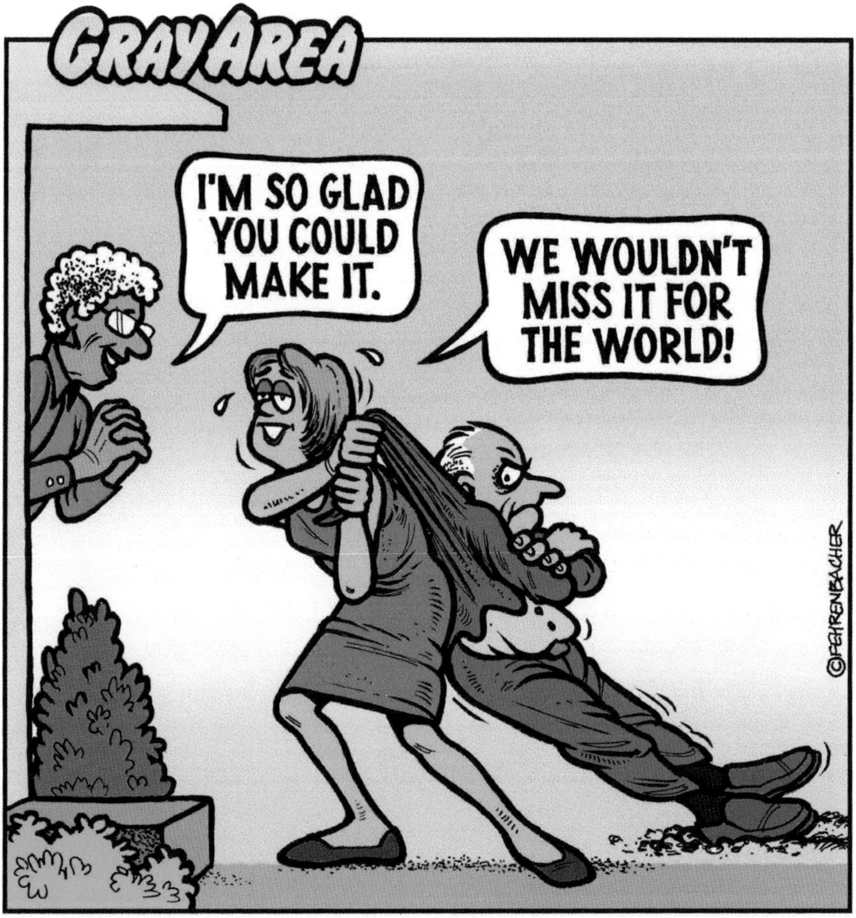
GRAY AREA
I'M SO GLAD YOU COULD MAKE IT.
WE WOULDN'T MISS IT FOR THE WORLD!
©FEHRENBACHER

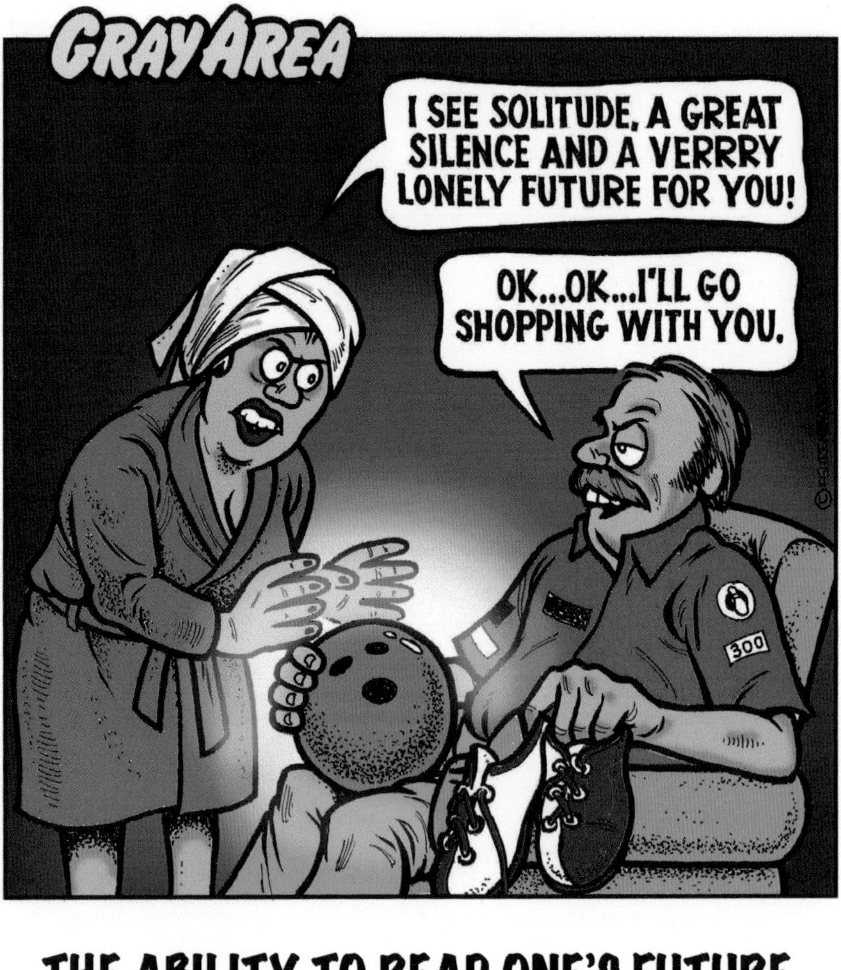
GRAY AREA
I SEE SOLITUDE, A GREAT SILENCE AND A VERRRY LONELY FUTURE FOR YOU!
OK...OK...I'LL GO SHOPPING WITH YOU.
300

THE ABILITY TO READ ONE'S FUTURE.

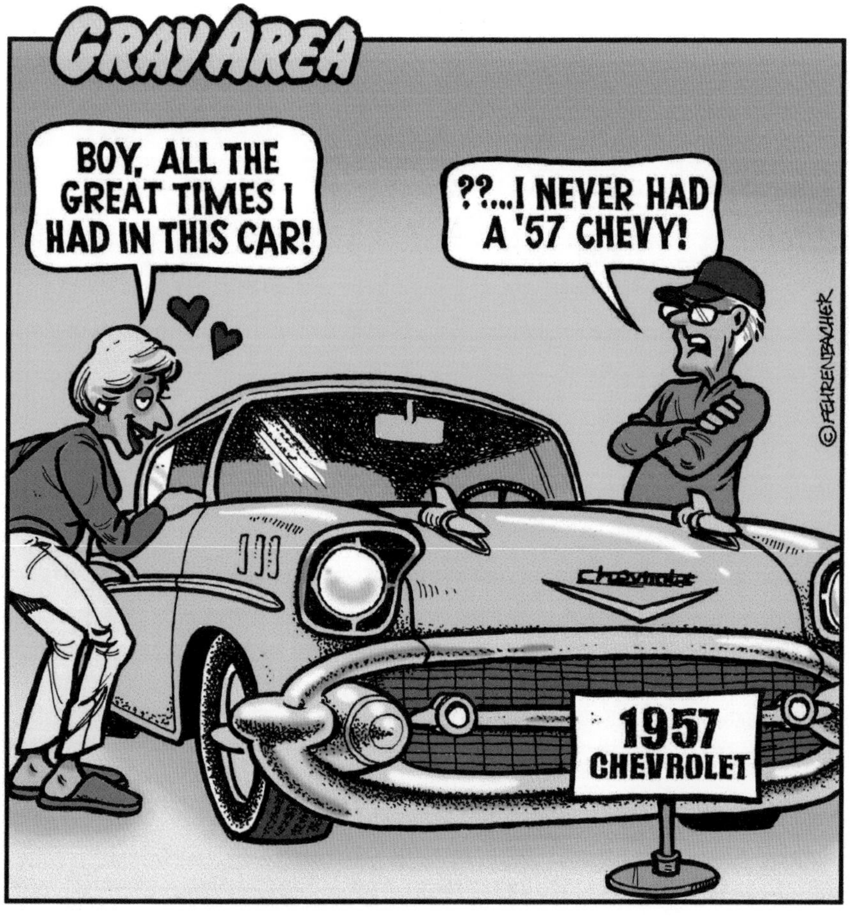
GRAY AREA
BOY, ALL THE GREAT TIMES I HAD IN THIS CAR!
??...I NEVER HAD A '57 CHEVY!
1957 CHEVROLET
©FEHRENBACHER

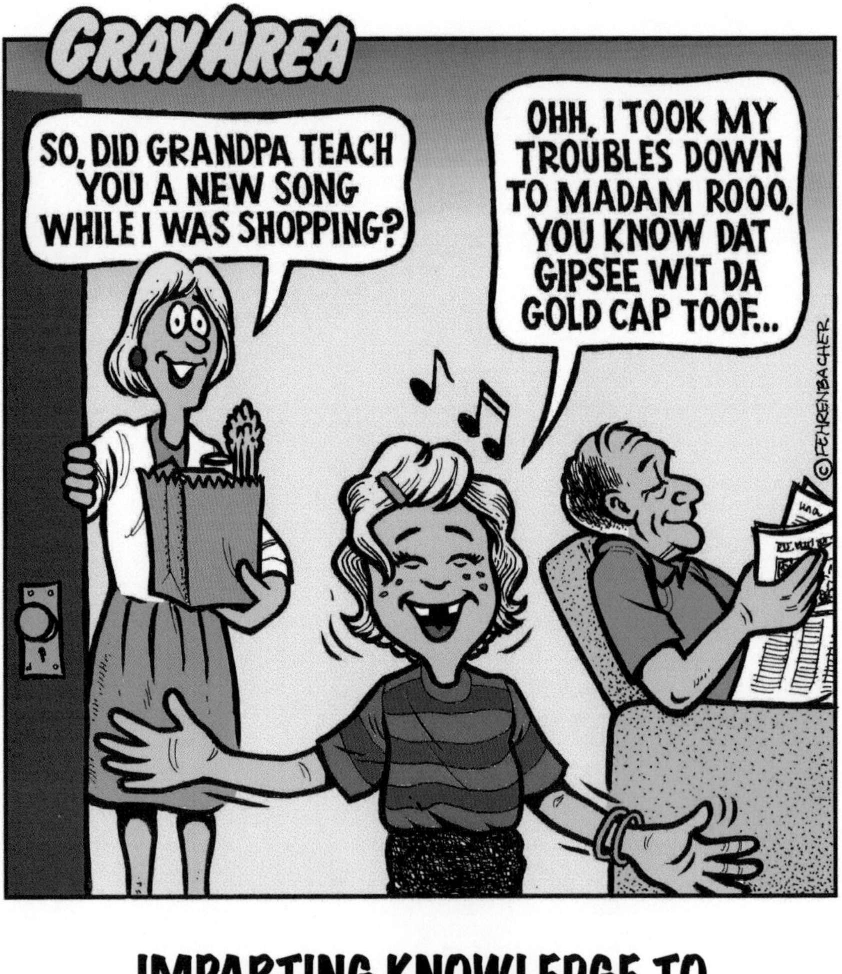
GRAY AREA
SO, DID GRANDPA TEACH YOU A NEW SONG WHILE I WAS SHOPPING?
OHH, I TOOK MY TROUBLES DOWN TO MADAM ROOO, YOU KNOW DAT GIPSEE WIT DA GOLD CAP TOOF...
© FEHRENBACHER

IMPARTING KNOWLEDGE TO A NEW GENERATION.

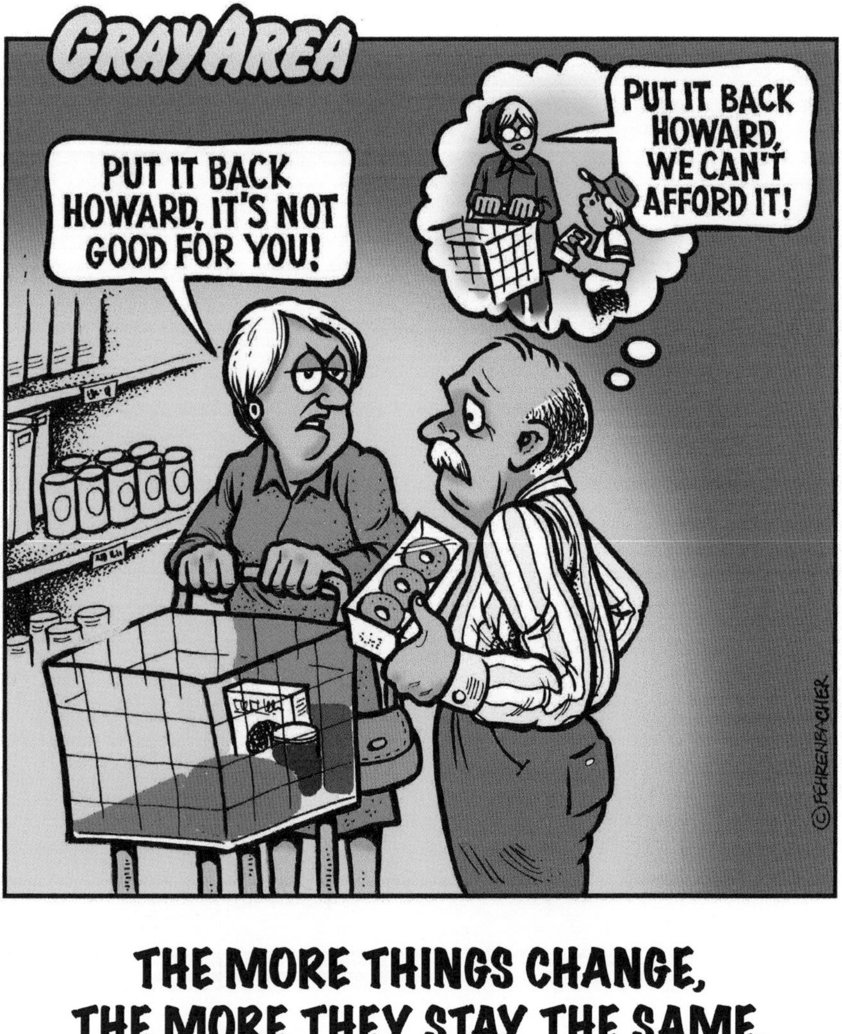
GRAY AREA
PUT IT BACK HOWARD, IT'S NOT GOOD FOR YOU!
PUT IT BACK HOWARD, WE CAN'T AFFORD IT!
©FEHRENBACHER

THE MORE THINGS CHANGE,
THE MORE THEY STAY THE SAME.

GRAY AREA
1975
DIAPER BAG
2016
RX
CPAP
DEPENDS
FiberBars
©FEHRENBACHER

**TAKING OVERNIGHT TRIPS...
STILL A HASSLE!**

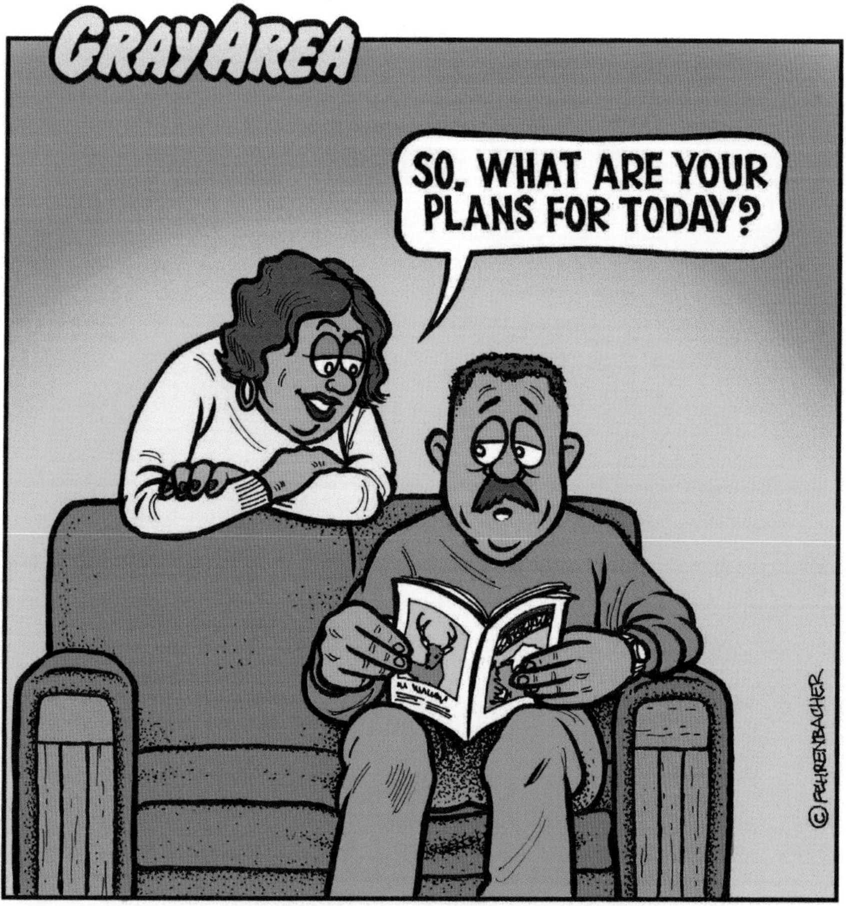
GRAY AREA
SO, WHAT ARE YOUR PLANS FOR TODAY?
© FEHRENBACHER

TRANSLATION:

WHAT *WERE* YOUR PLANS FOR TODAY?

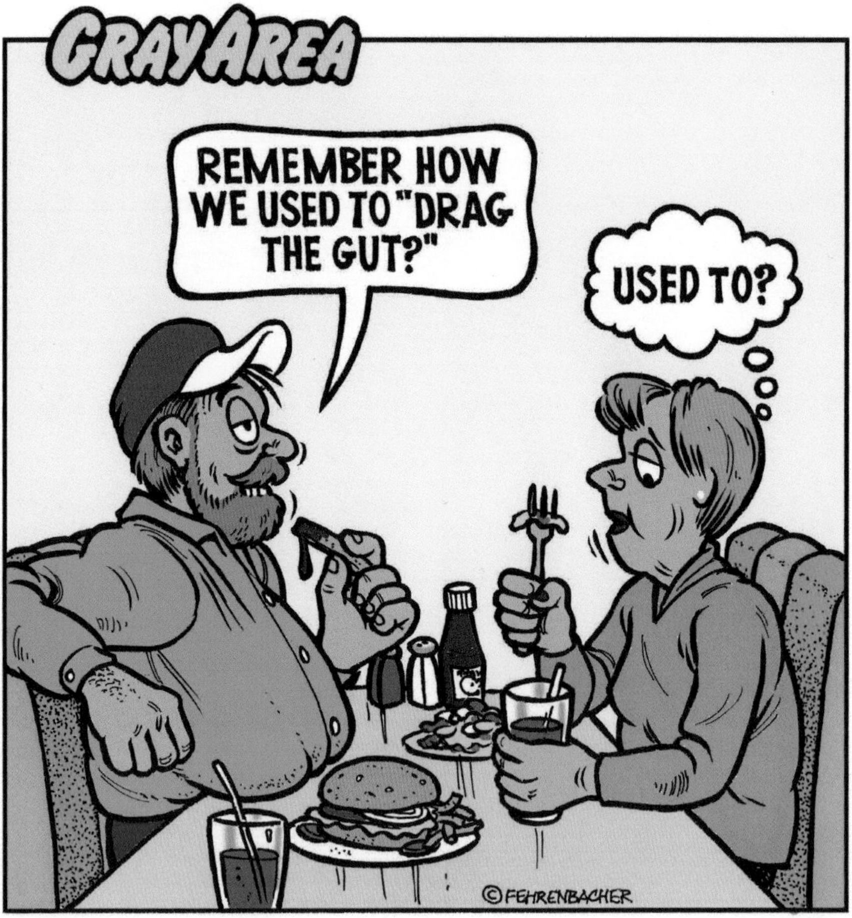
GRAY AREA
REMEMBER HOW WE USED TO "DRAG THE GUT?"
USED TO?
©FEHRENBACHER

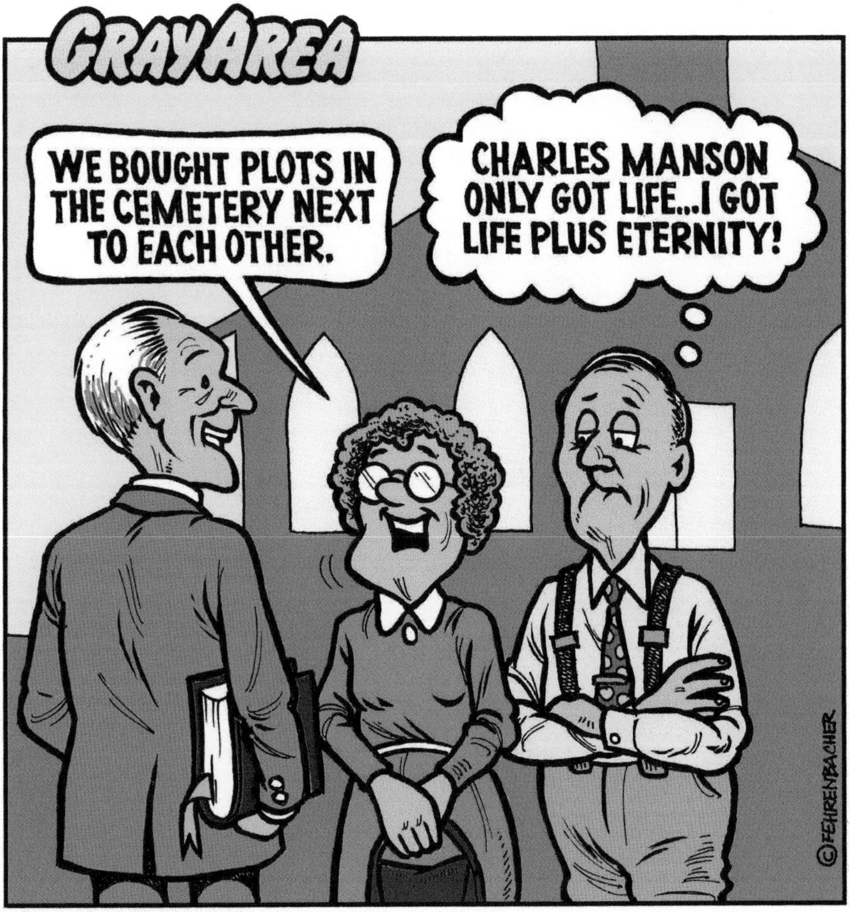
GRAY AREA
WE BOUGHT PLOTS IN THE CEMETERY NEXT TO EACH OTHER.
CHARLES MANSON ONLY GOT LIFE...I GOT LIFE PLUS ETERNITY!
©FEHRENBACHER

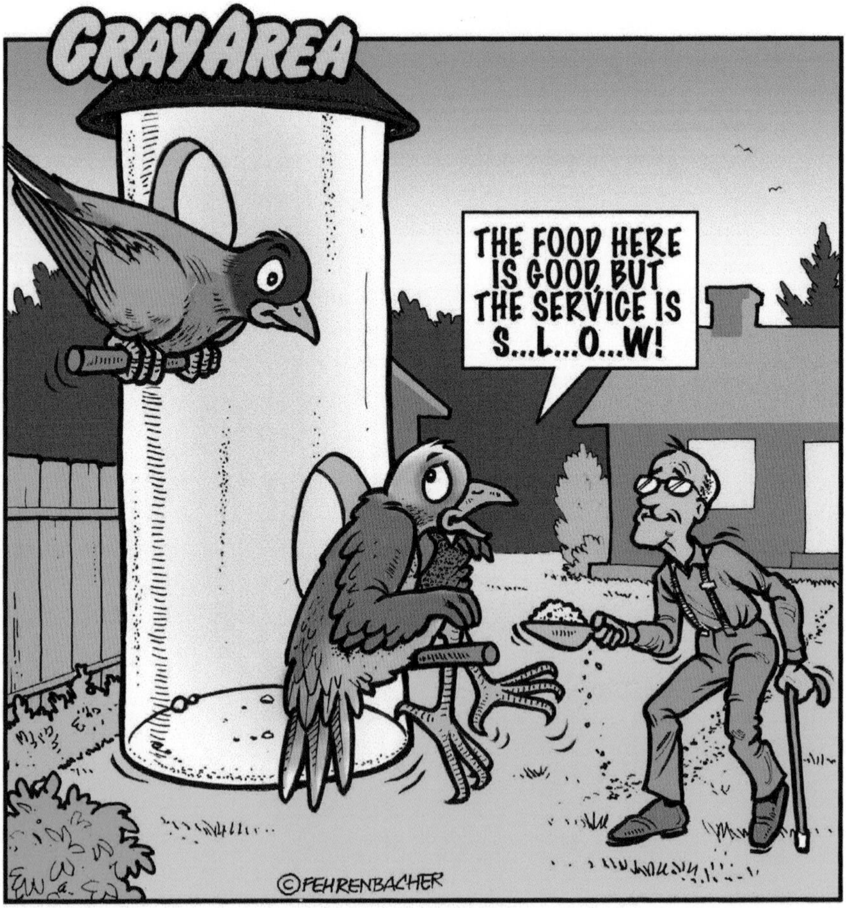
GRAY AREA
THE FOOD HERE IS GOOD, BUT THE SERVICE IS S...L...O...W!
©FEHRENBACHER

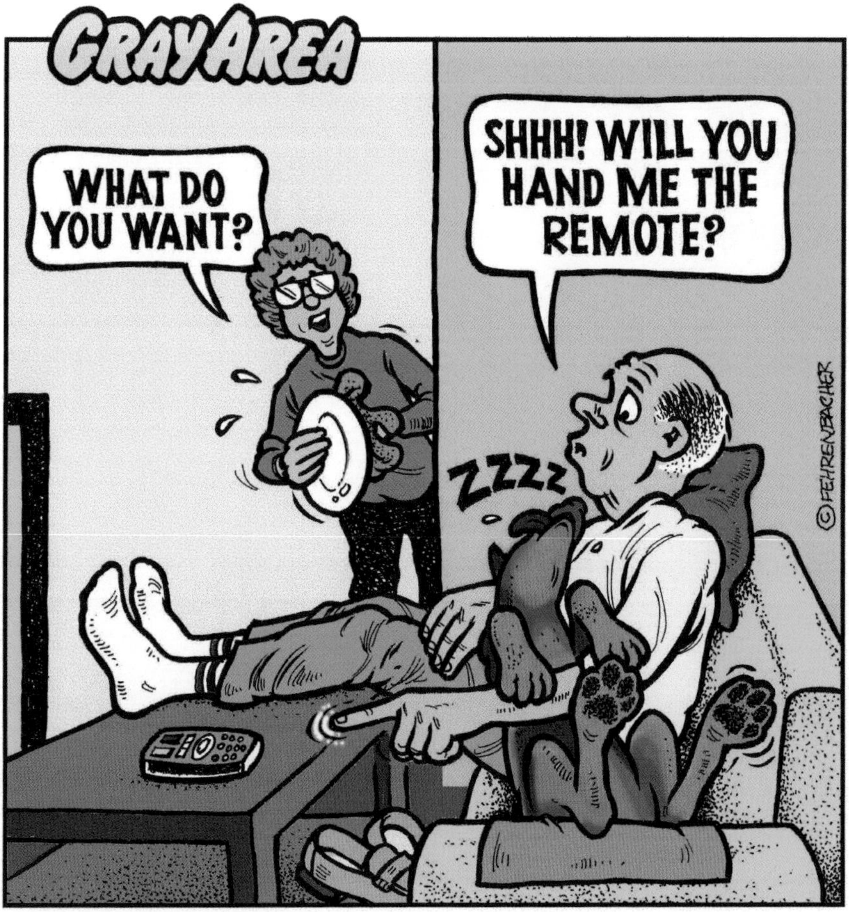
GRAY AREA
WHAT DO YOU WANT?
SHHH! WILL YOU HAND ME THE REMOTE?
ZZZZ
©FEHRENBACHER

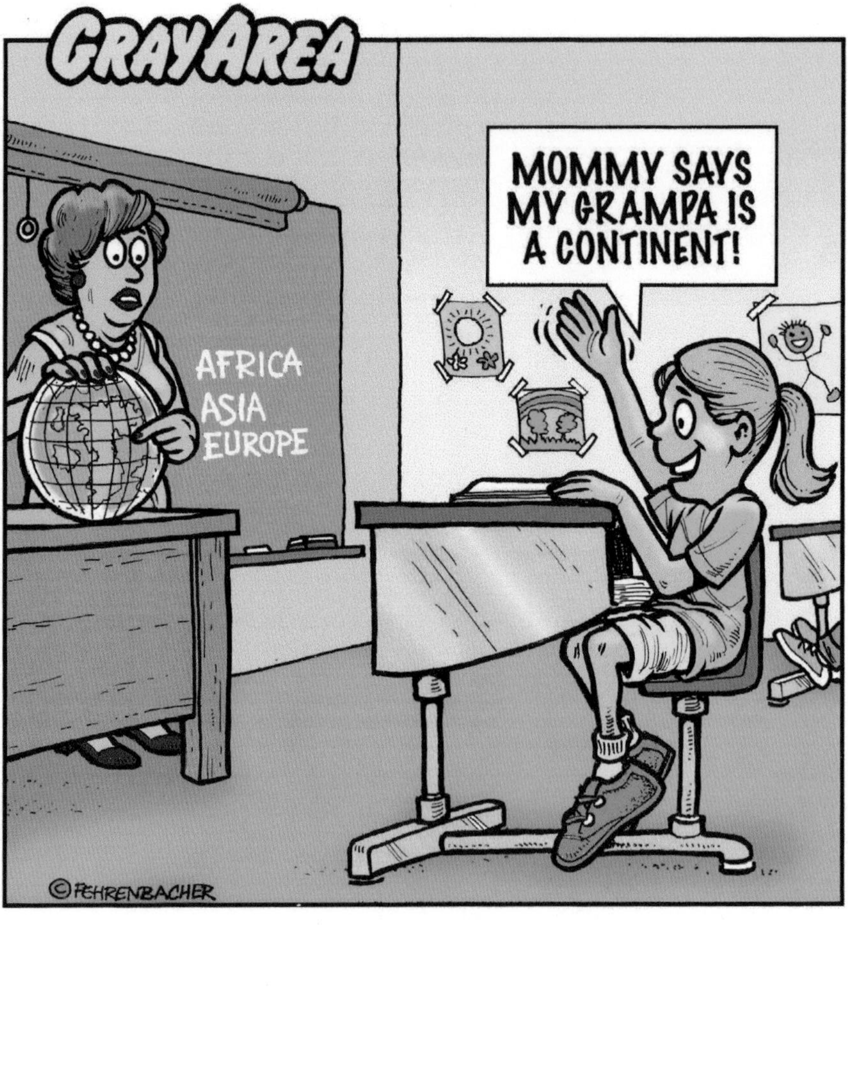
GRAY AREA
AFRICA
ASIA
EUROPE
MOMMY SAYS MY GRAMPA IS A CONTINENT!
©FEHRENBACHER

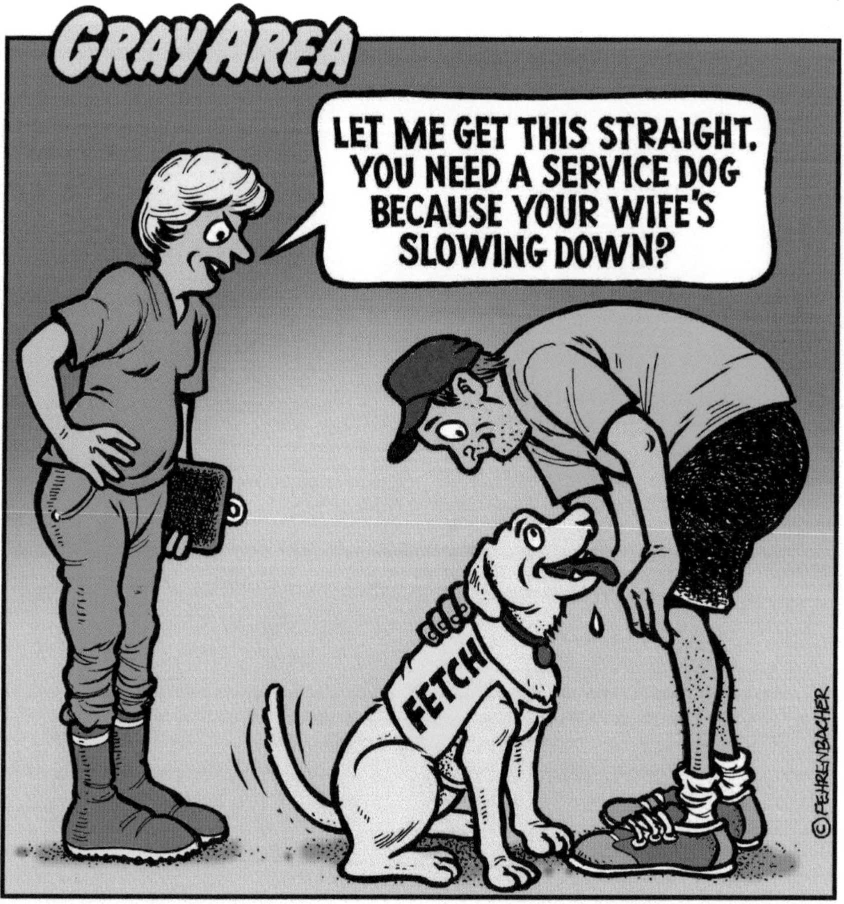
GRAY AREA
LET ME GET THIS STRAIGHT. YOU NEED A SERVICE DOG BECAUSE YOUR WIFE'S SLOWING DOWN?
FETCH
© FEHRENBACHER

GRAY AREA
PUT YOUR GLASSES ON, MEL. YOU JUST PLANTED A ROW OF M&Ms!
©FEHRENBACHER

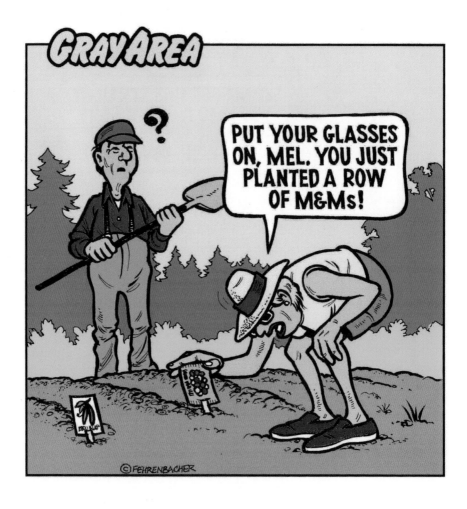

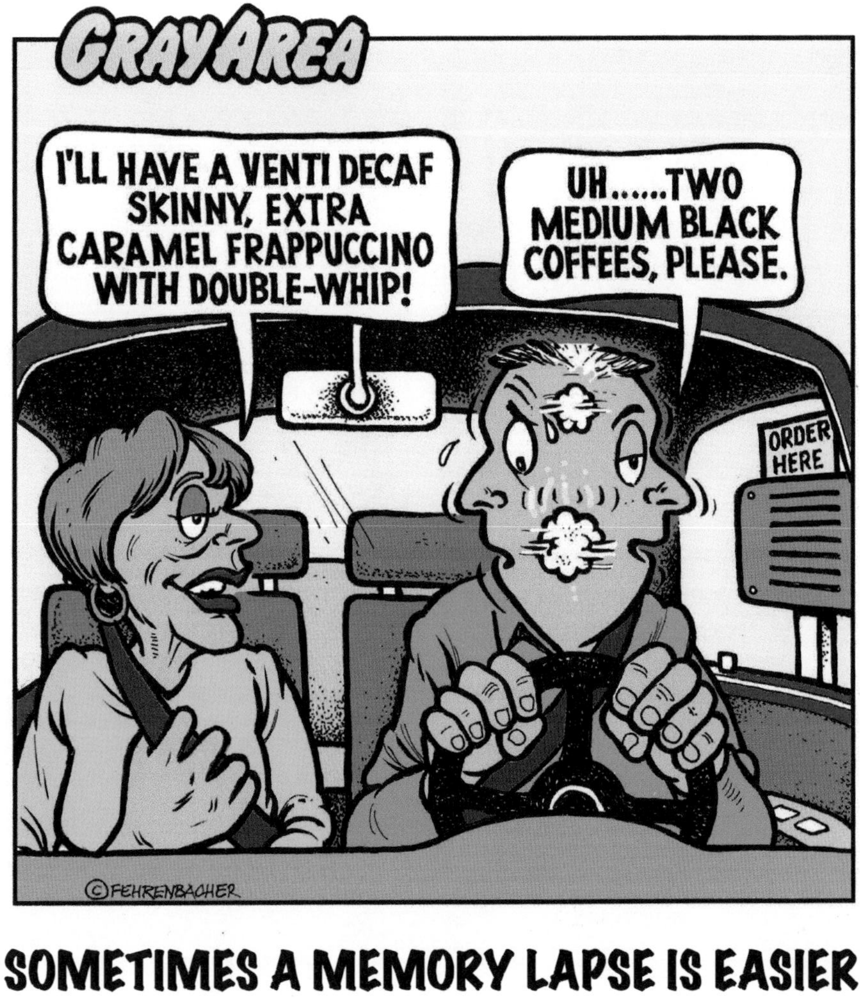
GRAY AREA
I'LL HAVE A VENTI DECAF SKINNY, EXTRA CARAMEL FRAPPUCCINO WITH DOUBLE-WHIP!
UH......TWO MEDIUM BLACK COFFEES, PLEASE.
ORDER HERE
©FEHRENBACHER

SOMETIMES A MEMORY LAPSE IS EASIER.

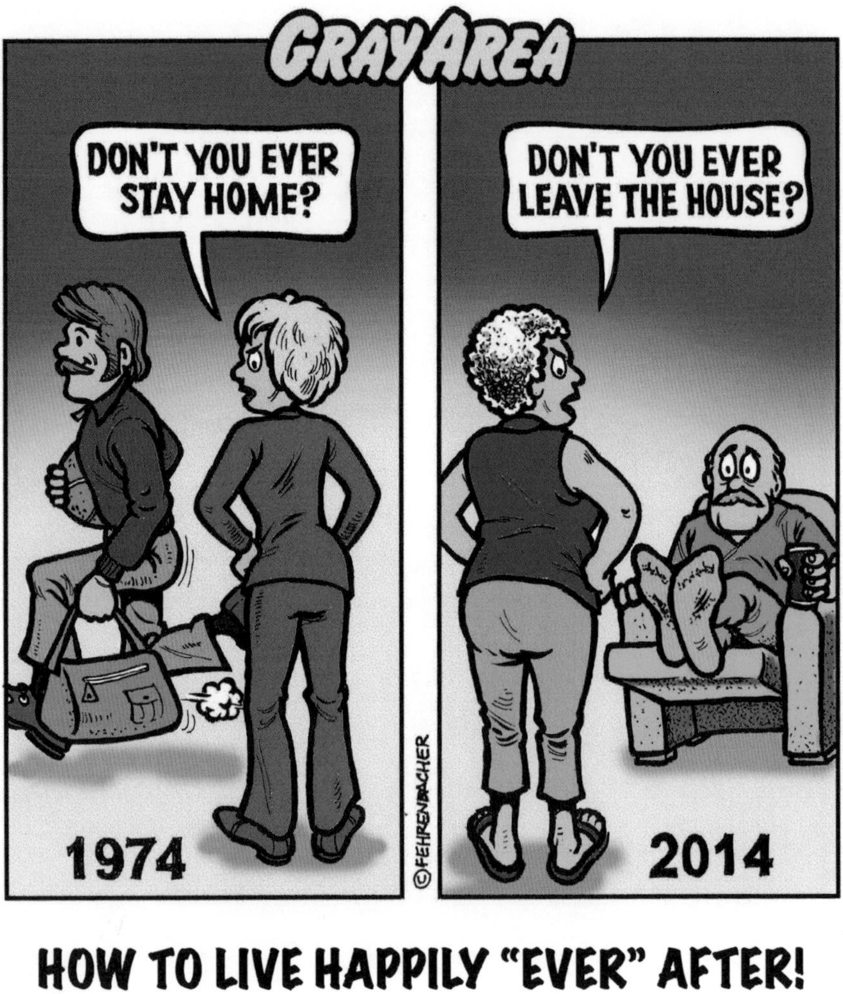
GRAY AREA
DON'T YOU EVER STAY HOME?
1974
DON'T YOU EVER LEAVE THE HOUSE?
2014
©FEHRENBACHER

HOW TO LIVE HAPPILY "EVER" AFTER!

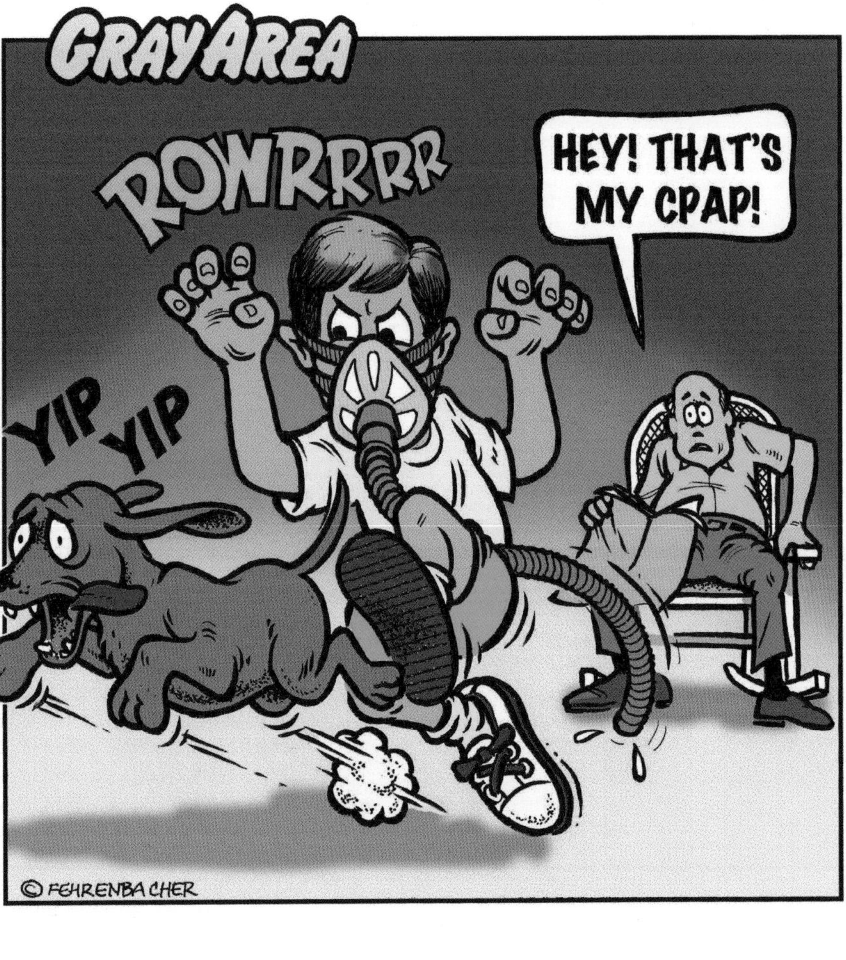
GRAY AREA
ROWRRRR
HEY! THAT'S MY CPAP!
YIP YIP
© FEHRENBACHER

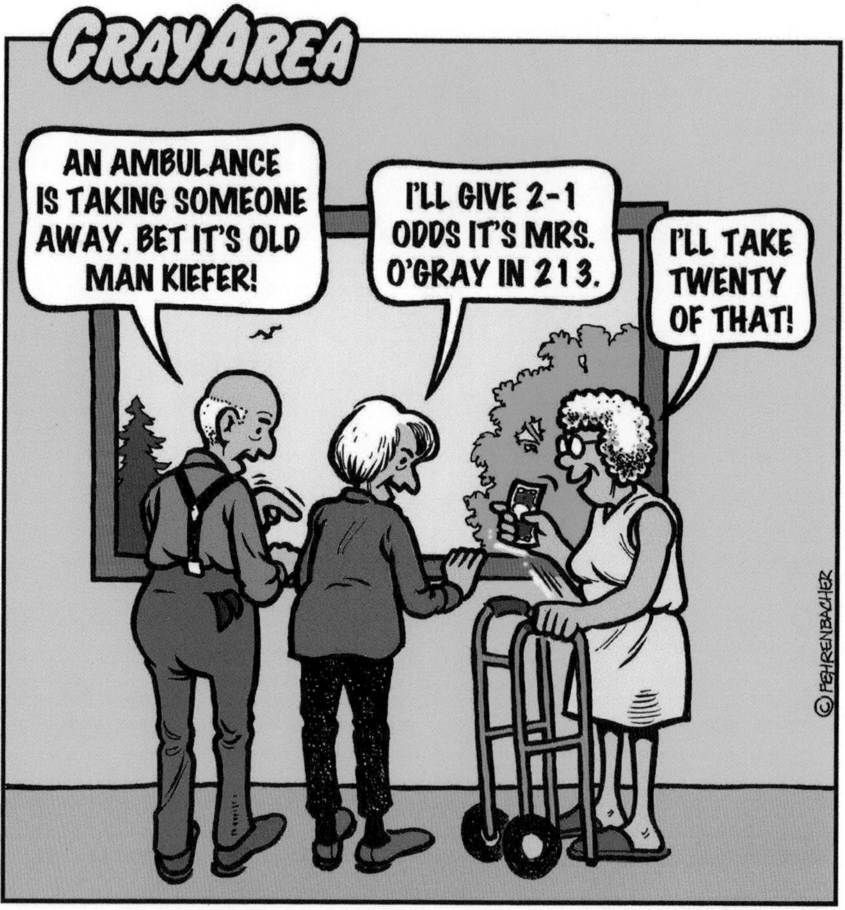
GRAYAREA
AN AMBULANCE IS TAKING SOMEONE AWAY. BET IT'S OLD MAN KIEFER!
I'LL GIVE 2-1 ODDS IT'S MRS. O'GRAY IN 213.
I'LL TAKE TWENTY OF THAT!
©FEHRENBACHER

KEEPING THEIR SPORTING SPIRIT ALIVE!

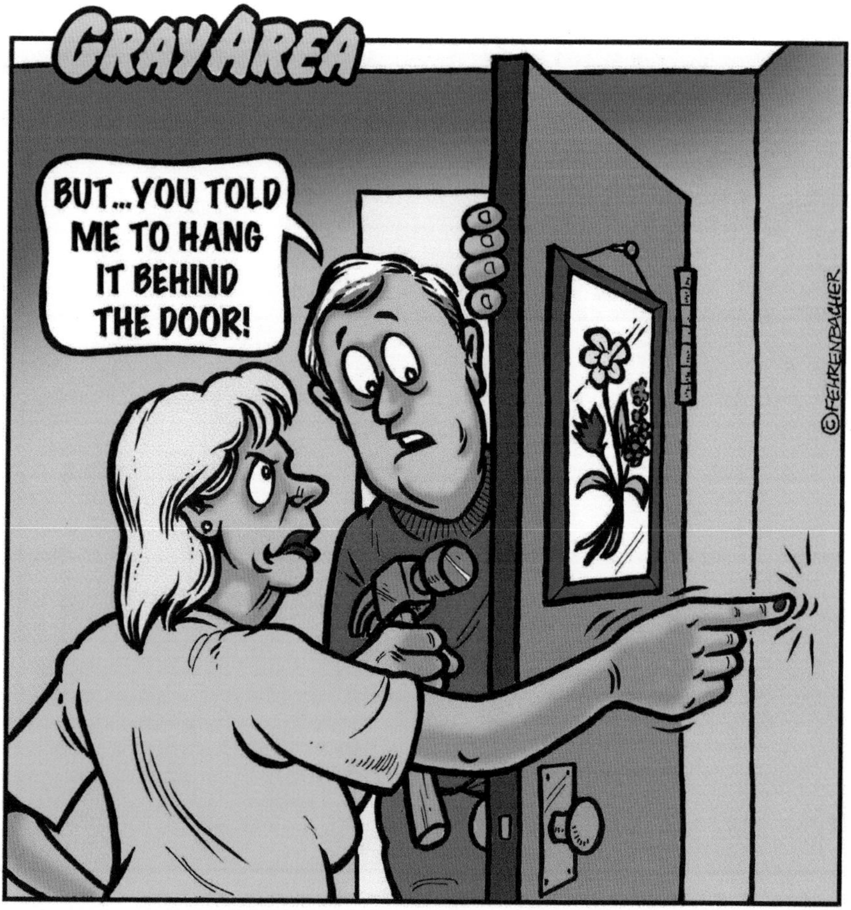
GRAY AREA
BUT...YOU TOLD ME TO HANG IT BEHIND THE DOOR!
©FEHRENBACHER

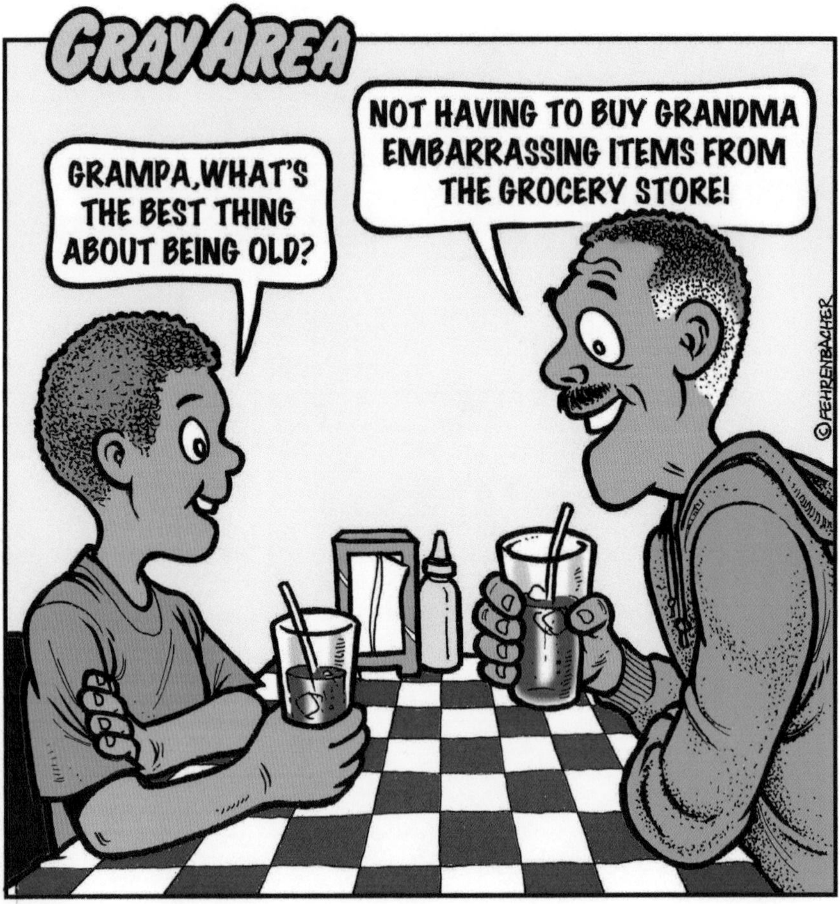
GRAY AREA
GRAMPA, WHAT'S THE BEST THING ABOUT BEING OLD?
NOT HAVING TO BUY GRANDMA EMBARRASSING ITEMS FROM THE GROCERY STORE!
©FEHRENBACHER

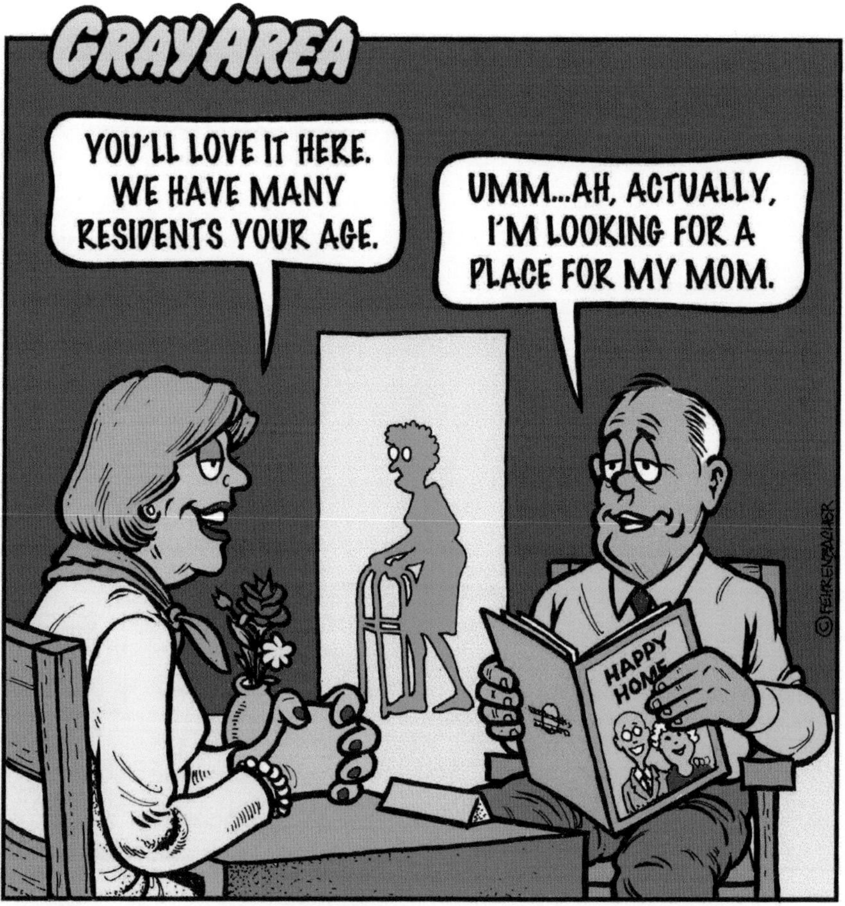
GRAY AREA
YOU'LL LOVE IT HERE. WE HAVE MANY RESIDENTS YOUR AGE.
UMM...AH, ACTUALLY, I'M LOOKING FOR A PLACE FOR MY MOM.
HAPPY HOME

THAT AWKWARD IN-BETWEEN AGE.

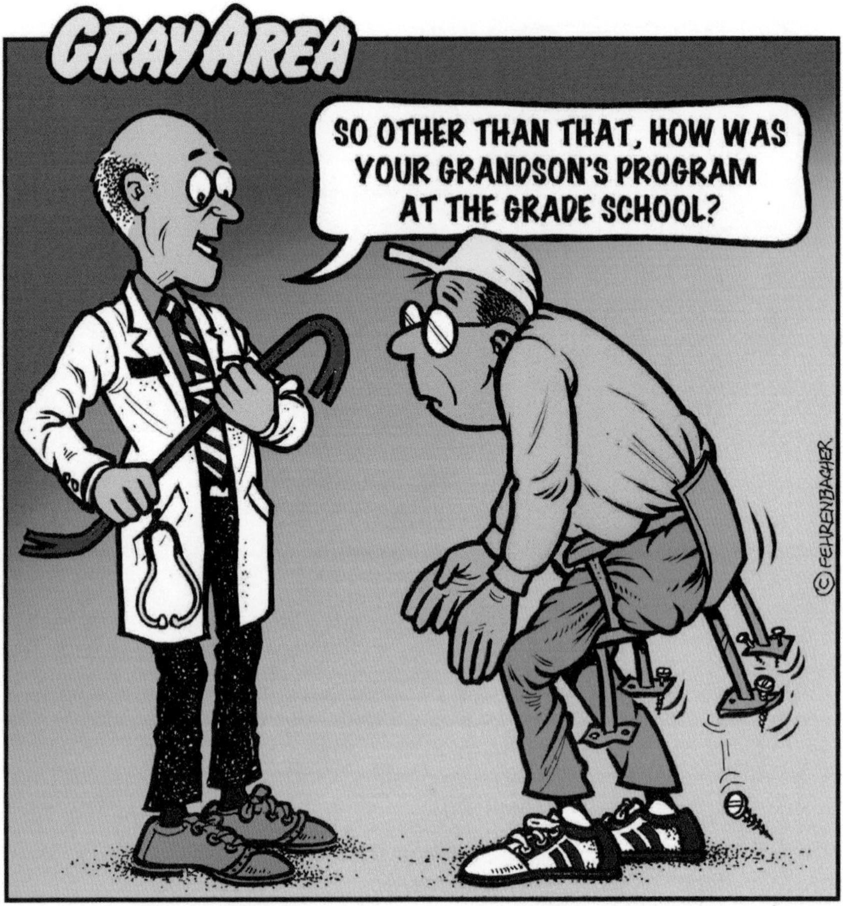
GRAY AREA
SO OTHER THAN THAT, HOW WAS YOUR GRANDSON'S PROGRAM AT THE GRADE SCHOOL?
© FEHRENBACHER

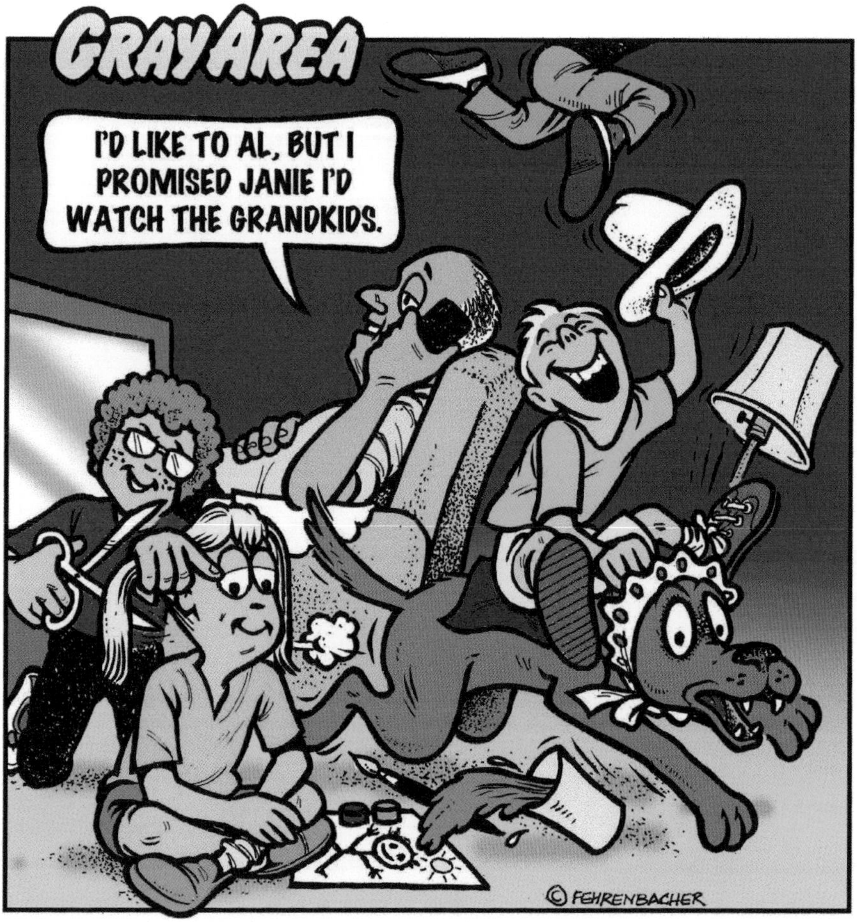
GRAY AREA
I'D LIKE TO AL, BUT I PROMISED JANIE I'D WATCH THE GRANDKIDS.
© FEHRENBACHER

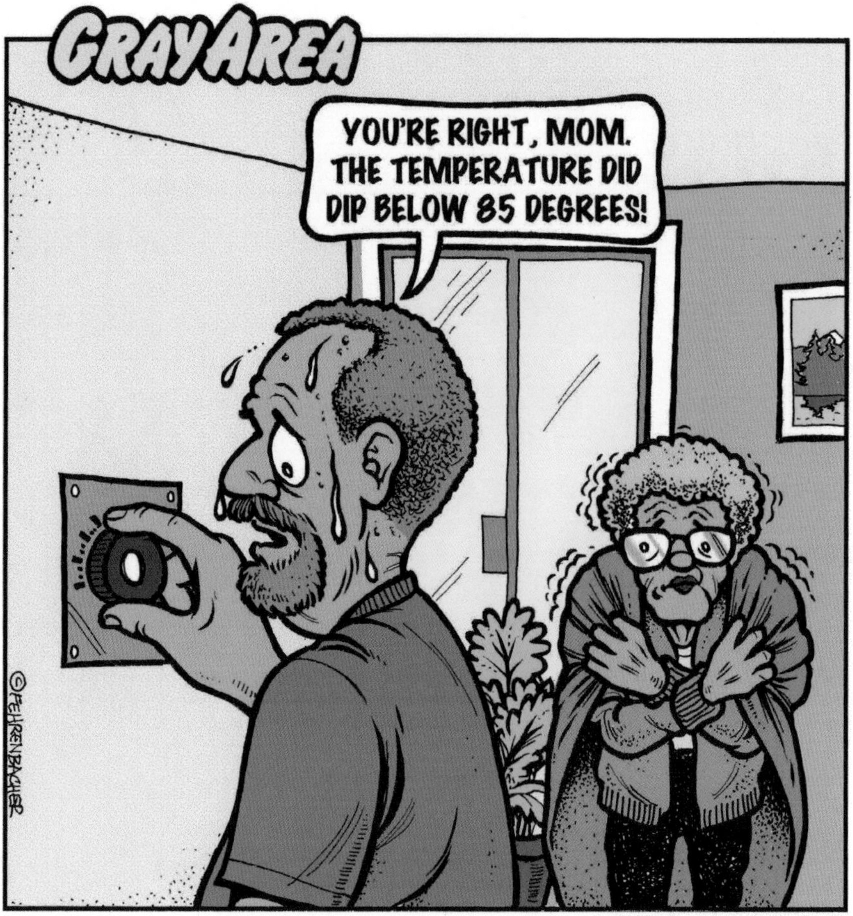
GRAY AREA
YOU'RE RIGHT, MOM. THE TEMPERATURE DID DIP BELOW 85 DEGREES!
©FEHRENBACHER

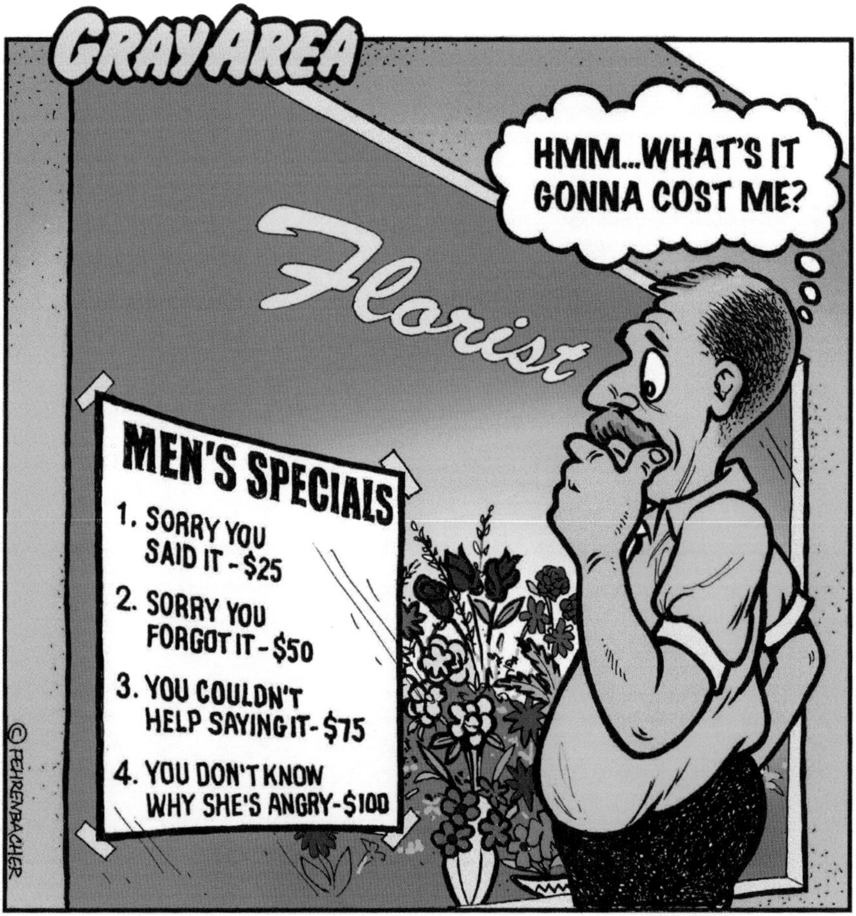
GRAY AREA
HMM...WHAT'S IT GONNA COST ME?
Florist
MEN'S SPECIALS
1. SORRY YOU SAID IT - $25
2. SORRY YOU FORGOT IT - $50
3. YOU COULDN'T HELP SAYING IT - $75
4. YOU DON'T KNOW WHY SHE'S ANGRY - $100
© FEHRENBACHER

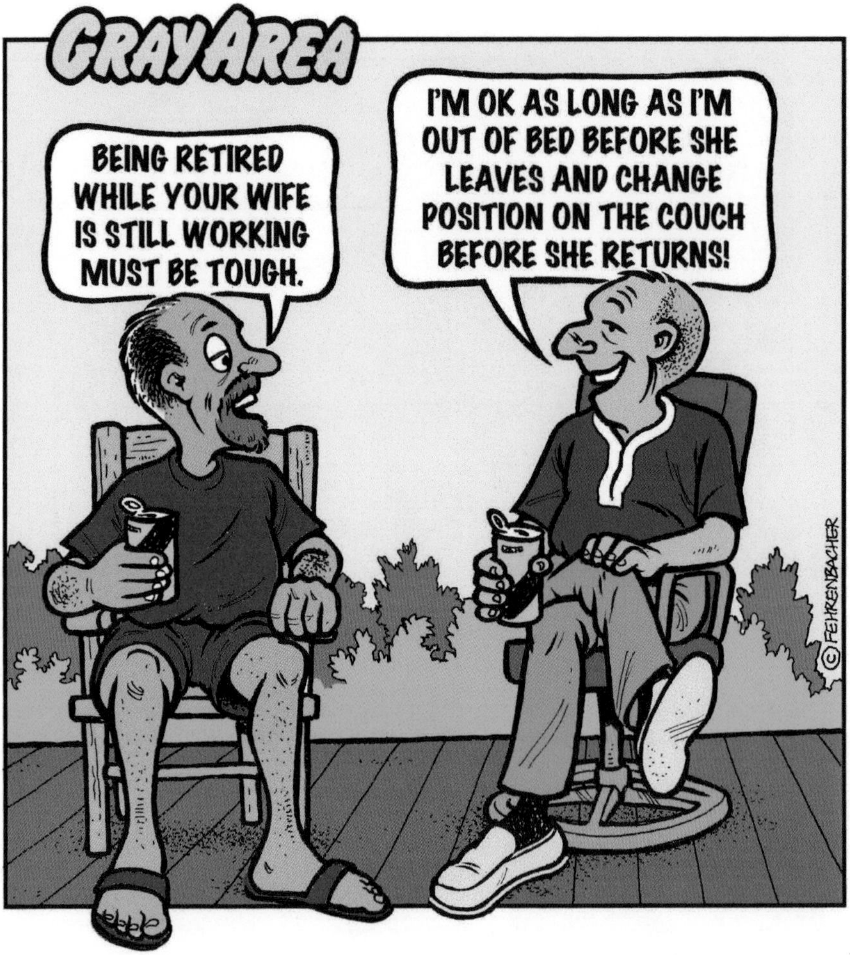
GRAYAREA
BEING RETIRED WHILE YOUR WIFE IS STILL WORKING MUST BE TOUGH.
I'M OK AS LONG AS I'M OUT OF BED BEFORE SHE LEAVES AND CHANGE POSITION ON THE COUCH BEFORE SHE RETURNS!
© FEHRENBACHER

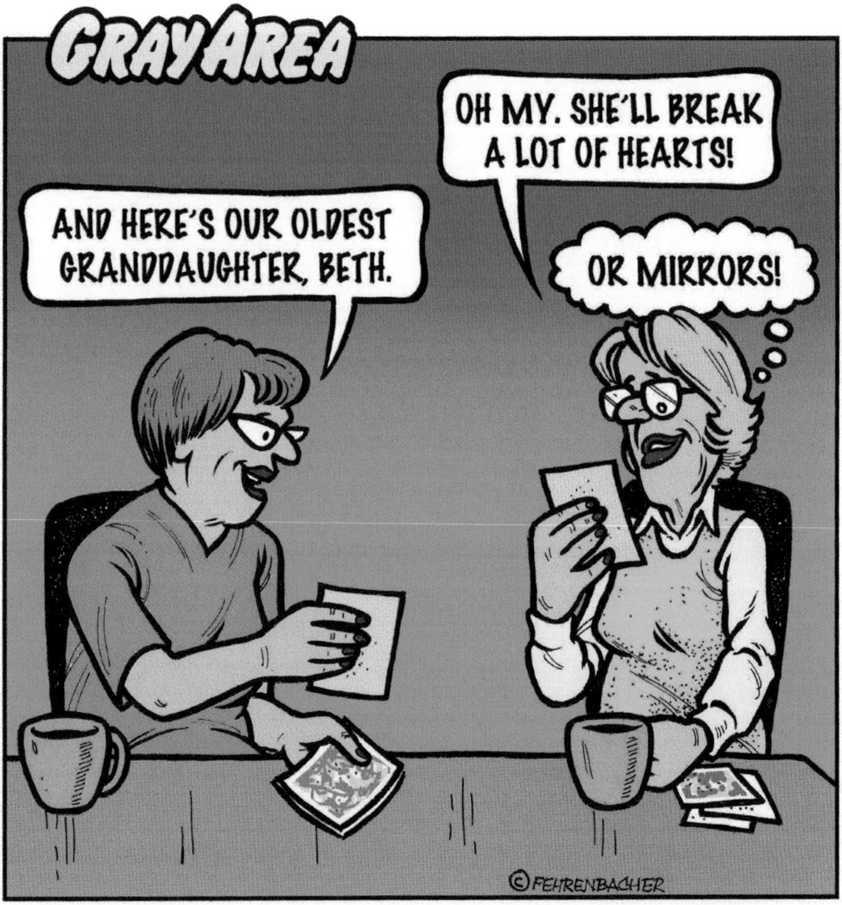
GRAY AREA
OH MY. SHE'LL BREAK A LOT OF HEARTS!
AND HERE'S OUR OLDEST GRANDDAUGHTER, BETH.
OR MIRRORS!
© FEHRENBACHER

KEEPING OLD FRIENDS TAKES TACT!

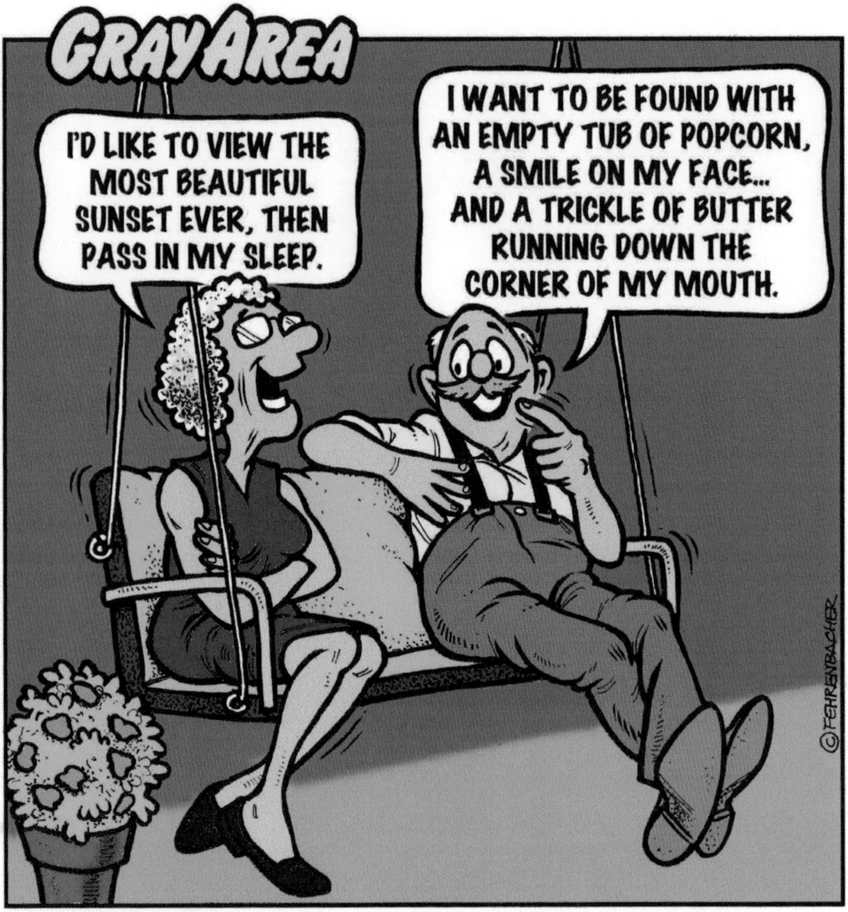
GRAY AREA
I'D LIKE TO VIEW THE MOST BEAUTIFUL SUNSET EVER, THEN PASS IN MY SLEEP.
I WANT TO BE FOUND WITH AN EMPTY TUB OF POPCORN, A SMILE ON MY FACE... AND A TRICKLE OF BUTTER RUNNING DOWN THE CORNER OF MY MOUTH.
©FEHRENBACHER

PLANNING ADVANCE DIRECTIVES.

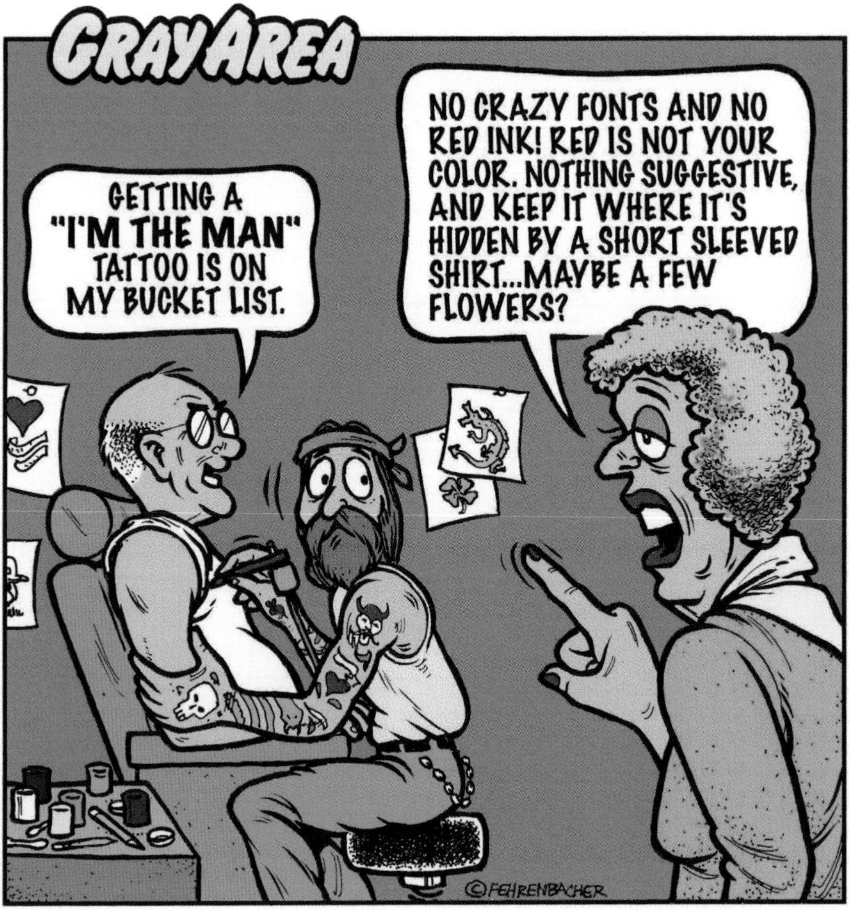
GRAY AREA
GETTING A "I'M THE MAN" TATTOO IS ON MY BUCKET LIST.
NO CRAZY FONTS AND NO RED INK! RED IS NOT YOUR COLOR. NOTHING SUGGESTIVE, AND KEEP IT WHERE IT'S HIDDEN BY A SHORT SLEEVED SHIRT...MAYBE A FEW FLOWERS?
©FEHRENBACHER

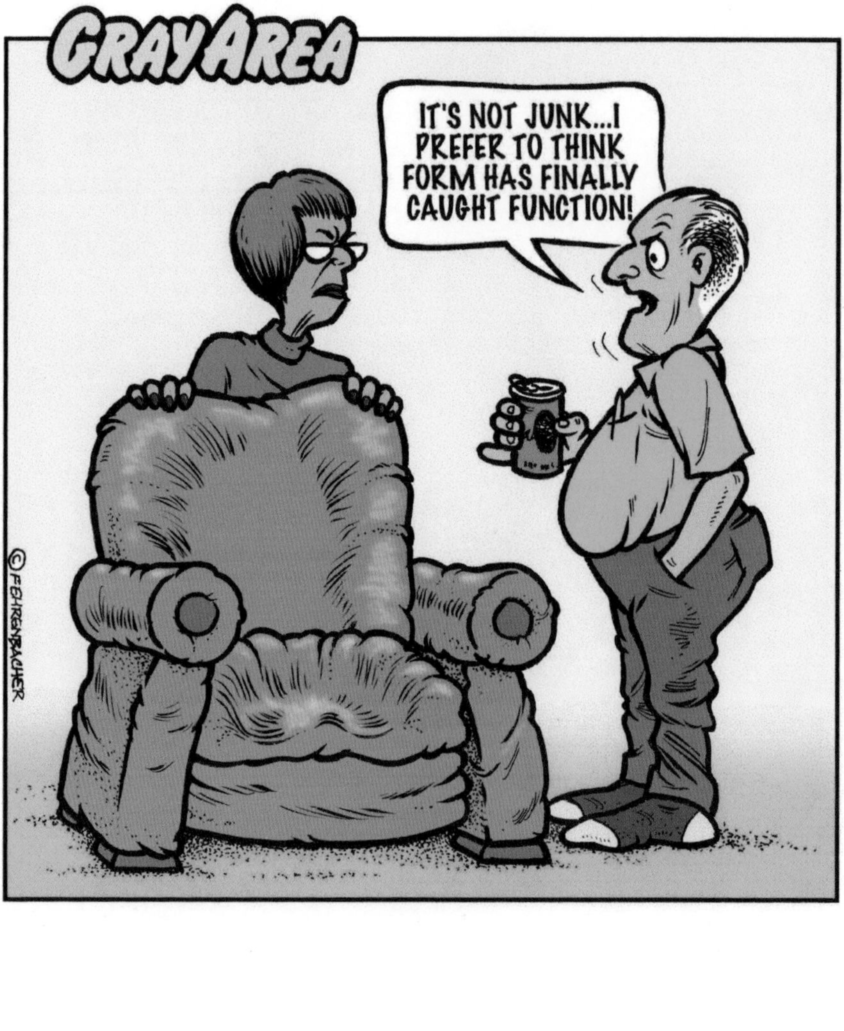
GRAYAREA
IT'S NOT JUNK...I PREFER TO THINK FORM HAS FINALLY CAUGHT FUNCTION!
© FEHRENBACHER

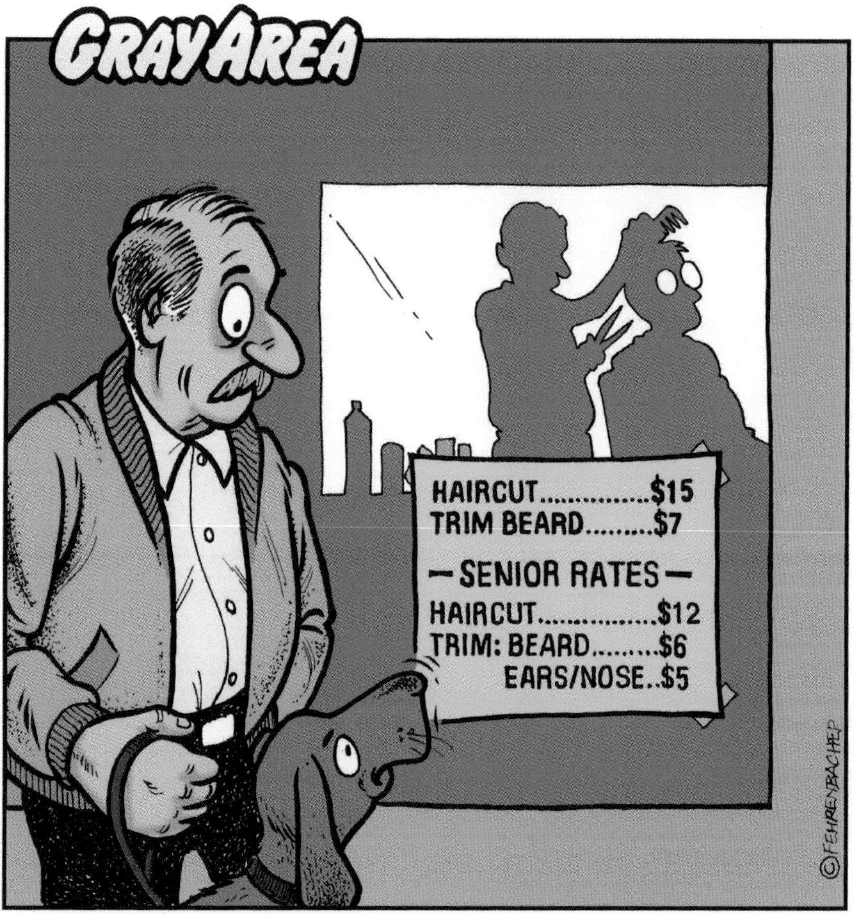
GRAY AREA
HAIRCUT................$15
TRIM BEARD.........$7
— SENIOR RATES —
HAIRCUT.................$12
TRIM: BEARD.........$6
EARS/NOSE..$5
©FEHRENBACHER

HARVESTING "OLD GROWTH."

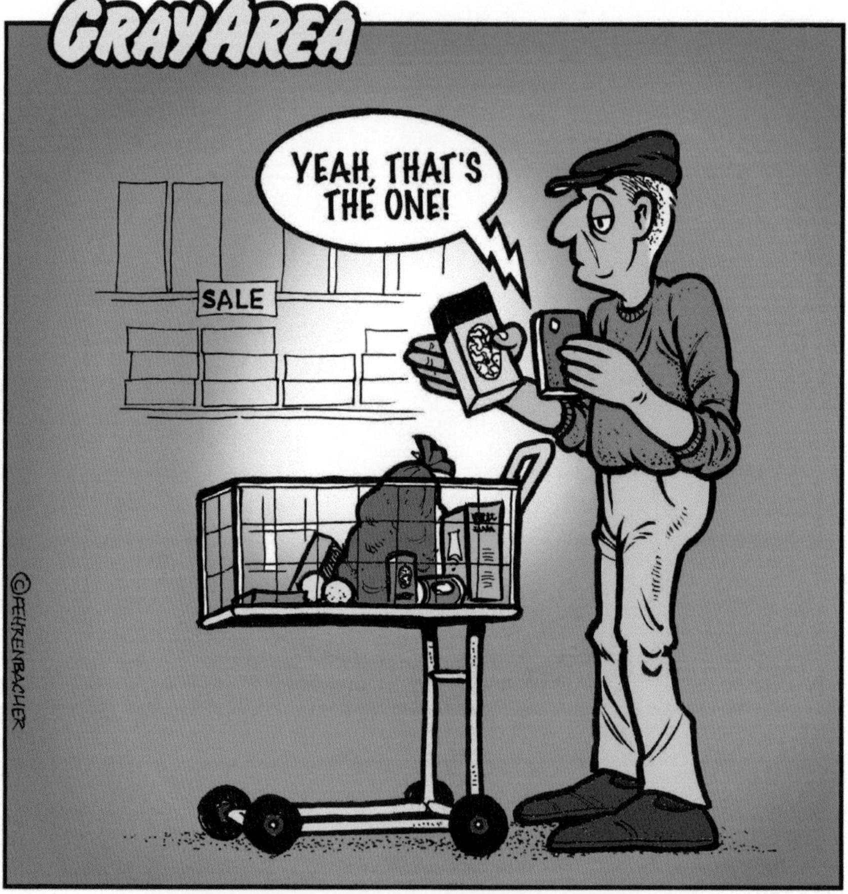
GRAY AREA
YEAH, THAT'S THE ONE!
SALE
©FEHRENBACHER

PRESSING THE ENVELOPE OF MODERN TECHNOLOGY!

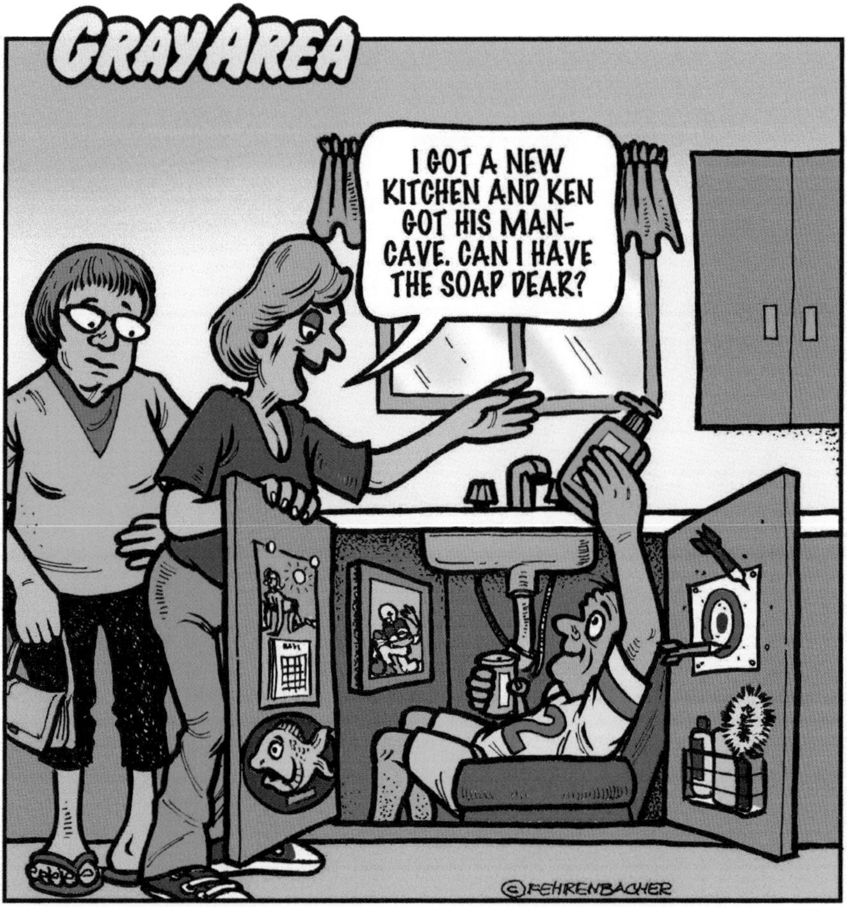
GRAY AREA
I GOT A NEW KITCHEN AND KEN GOT HIS MAN-CAVE. CAN I HAVE THE SOAP DEAR?
©FEHRENBACHER

LEARNING HOW TO COMPROMISE.

GRAY AREA
WELL, YOU'RE THE ONE WHO WANTED MEMORY FOAM!
ACK ACK
©FEHRENBACHER

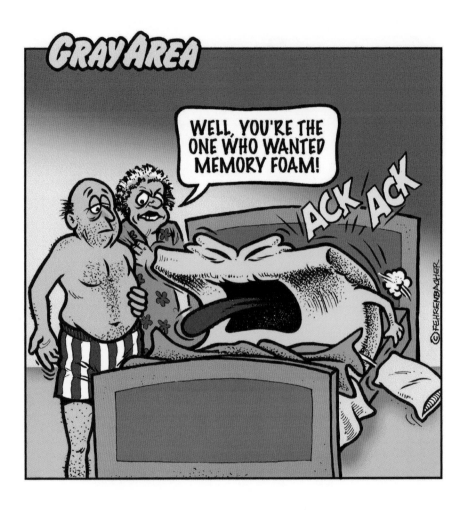

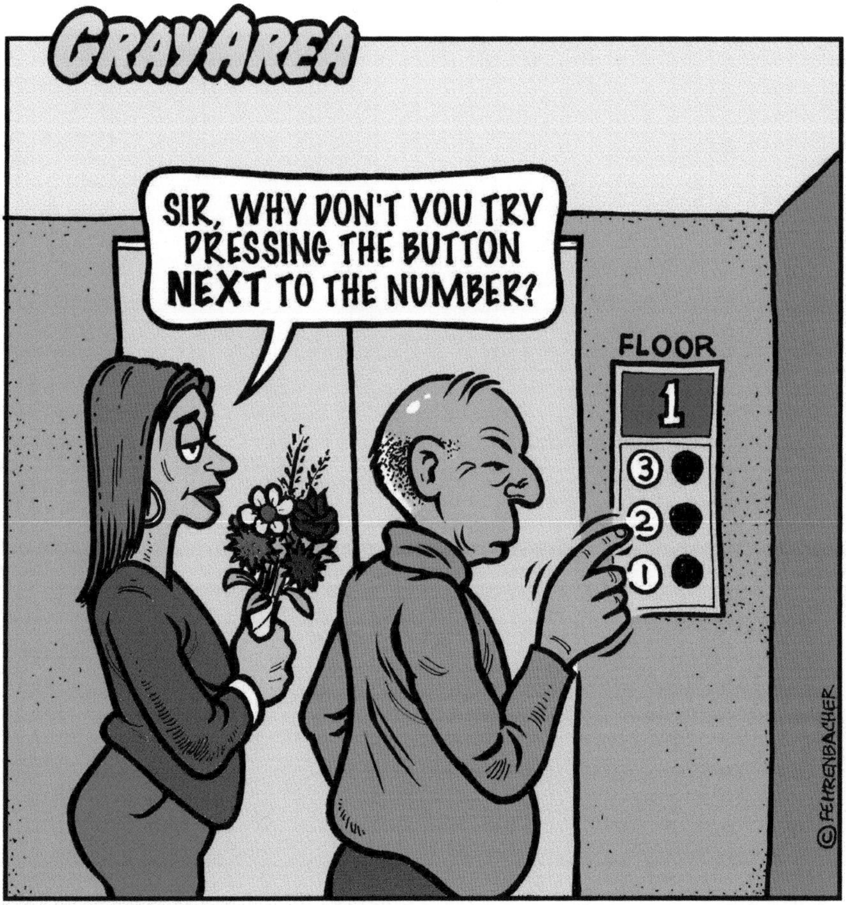
GRAY AREA
SIR, WHY DON'T YOU TRY PRESSING THE BUTTON NEXT TO THE NUMBER?
FLOOR
1
3
2
1
© FEHRENBACHER

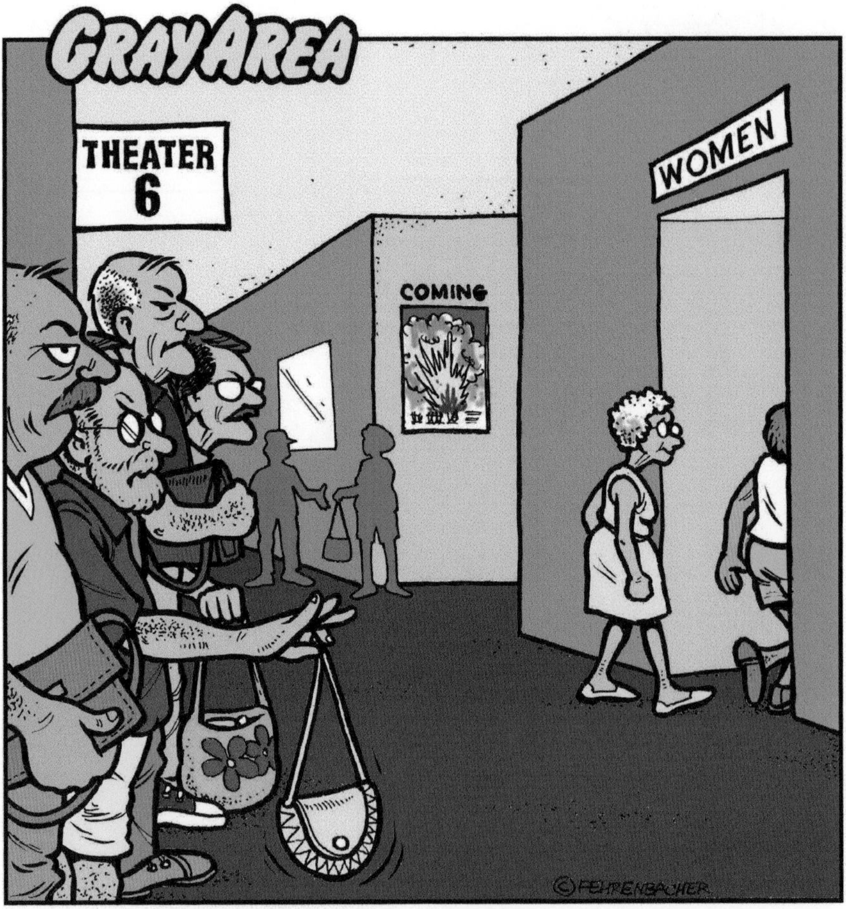
GRAY AREA
THEATER 6
COMING
WOMEN
©FEHRENBACHER

THE POST-MOVIE "LONG GRAY LINE."

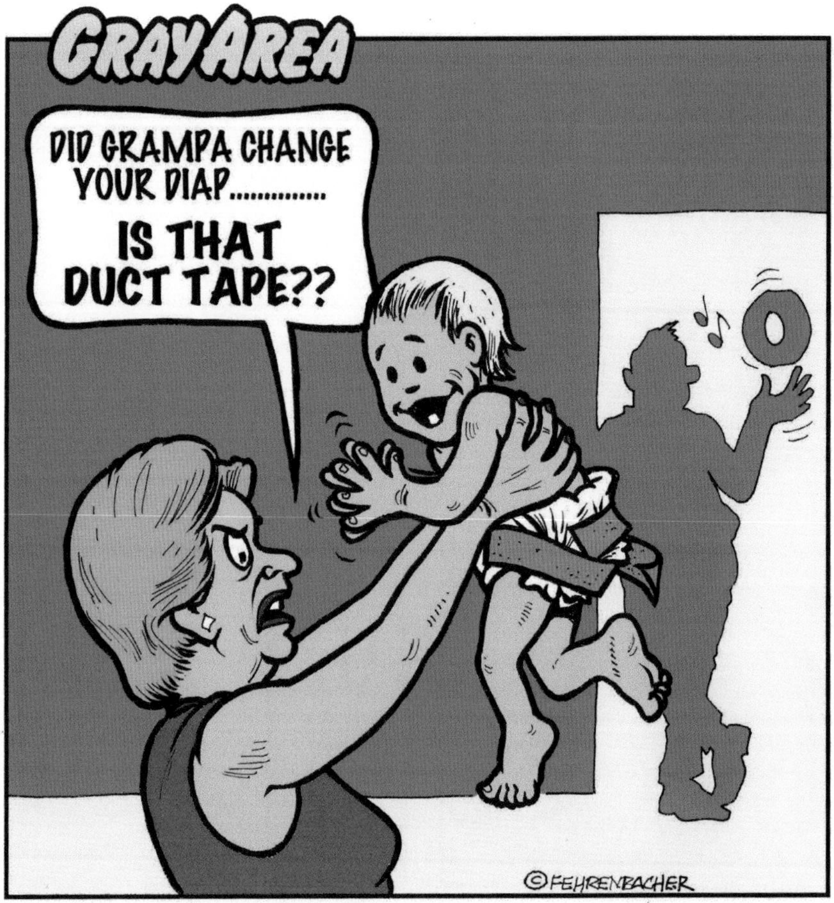
GRAY AREA
DID GRAMPA CHANGE YOUR DIAP..............
IS THAT DUCT TAPE??
©FEHRENBACHER

THE ABILITY TO ADAPT...OVERCOME!

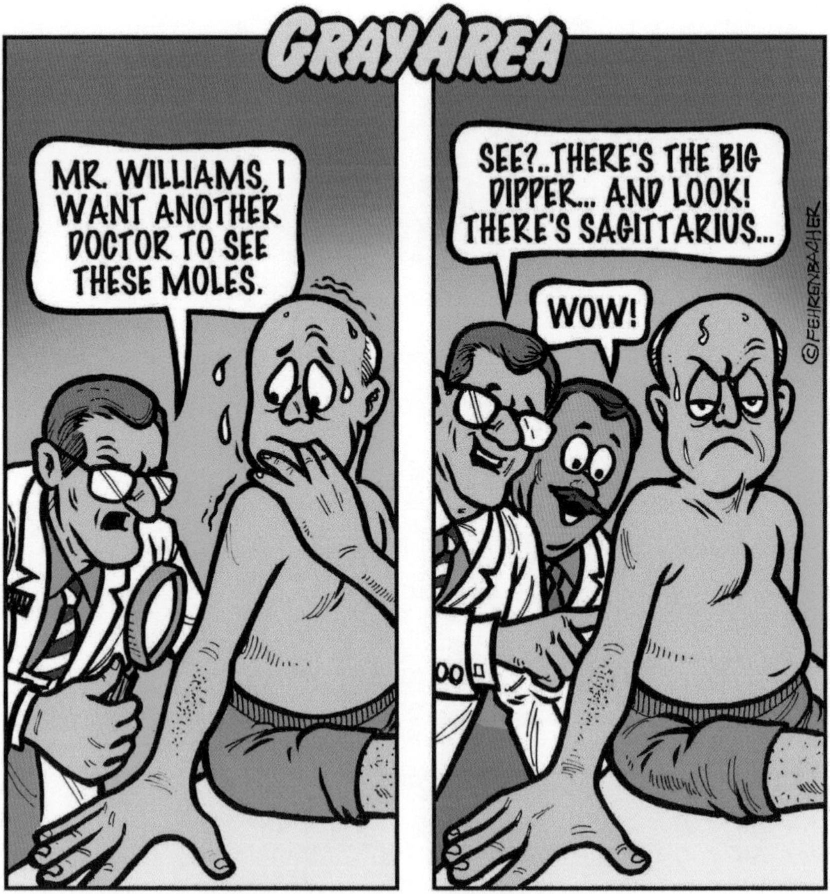
GRAY AREA
MR. WILLIAMS, I WANT ANOTHER DOCTOR TO SEE THESE MOLES.
SEE?..THERE'S THE BIG DIPPER... AND LOOK! THERE'S SAGITTARIUS...
WOW!
©FEHRENBACHER

DOCTORS AGREE THAT SENIORS WORRY TOO MUCH!

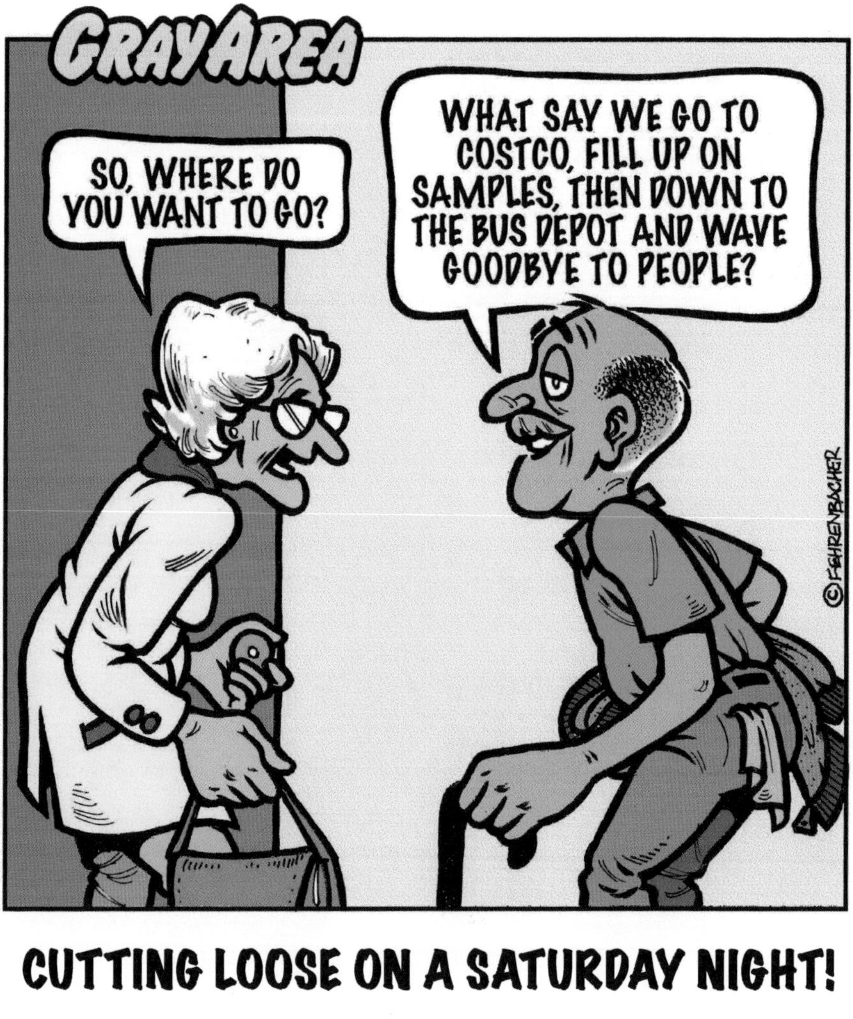
GRAY AREA
SO, WHERE DO YOU WANT TO GO?
WHAT SAY WE GO TO COSTCO, FILL UP ON SAMPLES, THEN DOWN TO THE BUS DEPOT AND WAVE GOODBYE TO PEOPLE?
© FAHRENBACHER

CUTTING LOOSE ON A SATURDAY NIGHT!

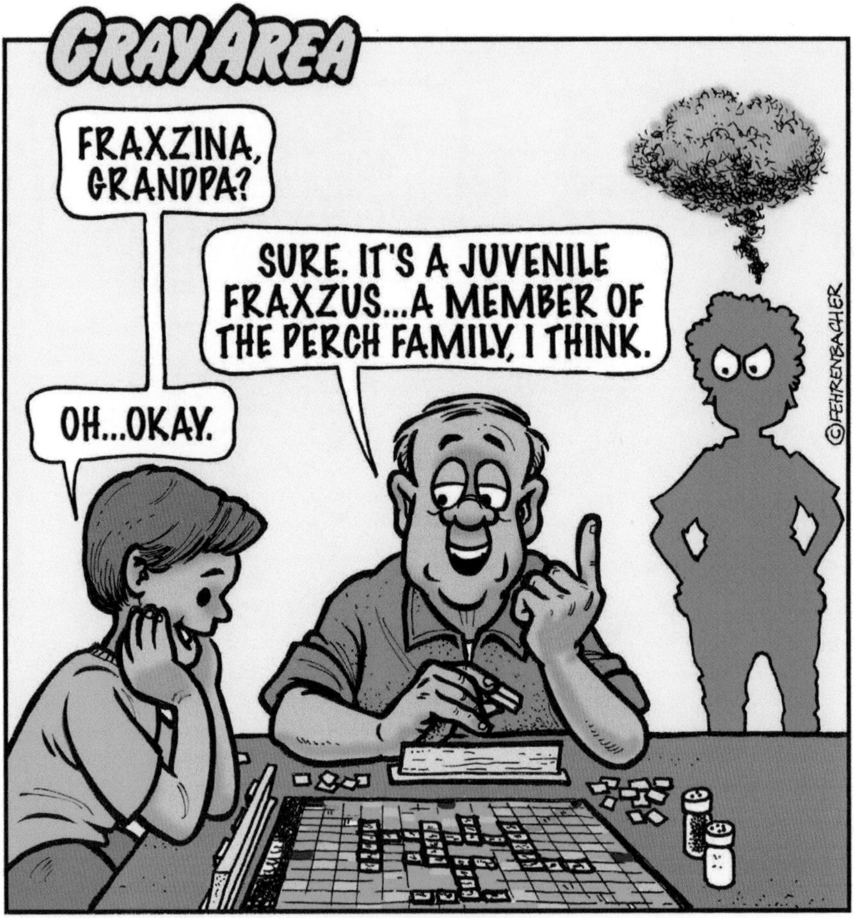
GRAY AREA
FRAXZINA, GRANDPA?
SURE. IT'S A JUVENILE FRAXZUS...A MEMBER OF THE PERCH FAMILY, I THINK.
OH...OKAY.
©FEHRENBACHER

SCRABBLE:
A GREAT LEARNING TOOL...SOMETIMES!

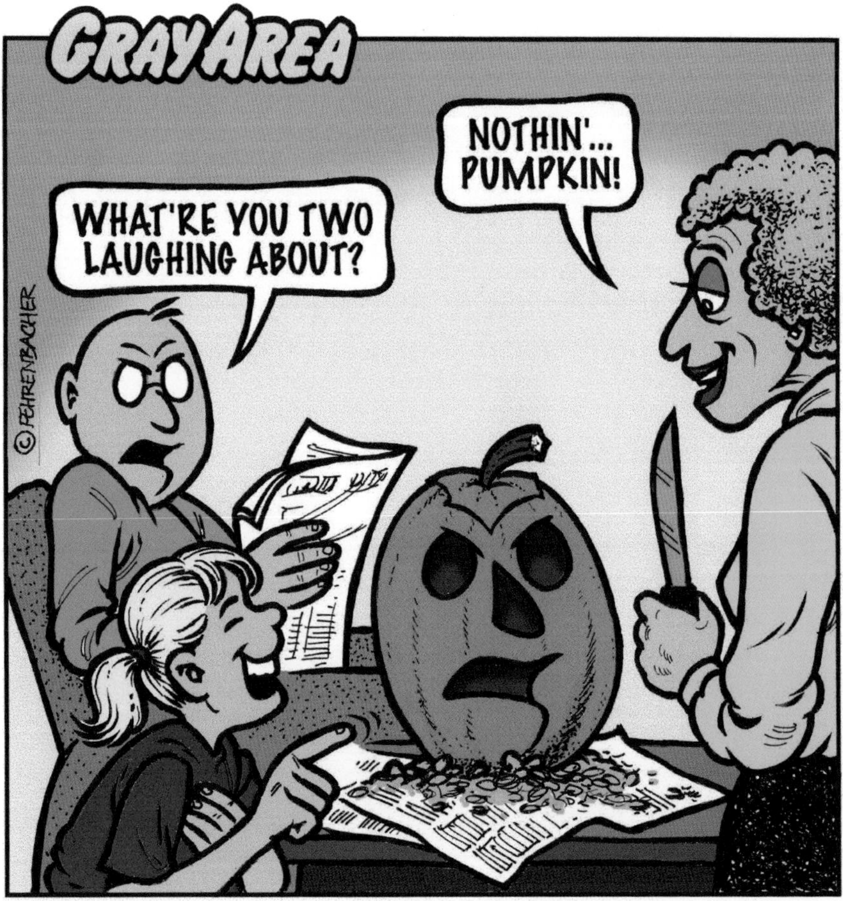
GRAY AREA
WHAT'RE YOU TWO LAUGHING ABOUT?
NOTHIN'... PUMPKIN!
© FEHRENBACHER

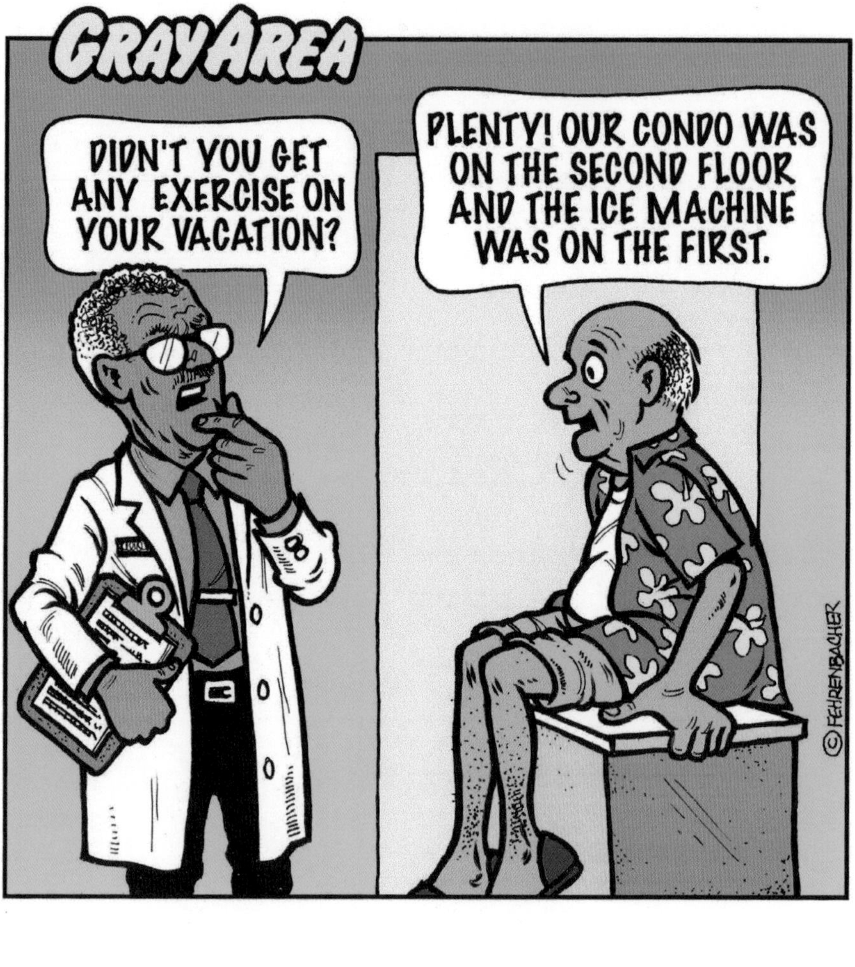
GRAY AREA
DIDN'T YOU GET ANY EXERCISE ON YOUR VACATION?
PLENTY! OUR CONDO WAS ON THE SECOND FLOOR AND THE ICE MACHINE WAS ON THE FIRST.
© FEHRENBACHER

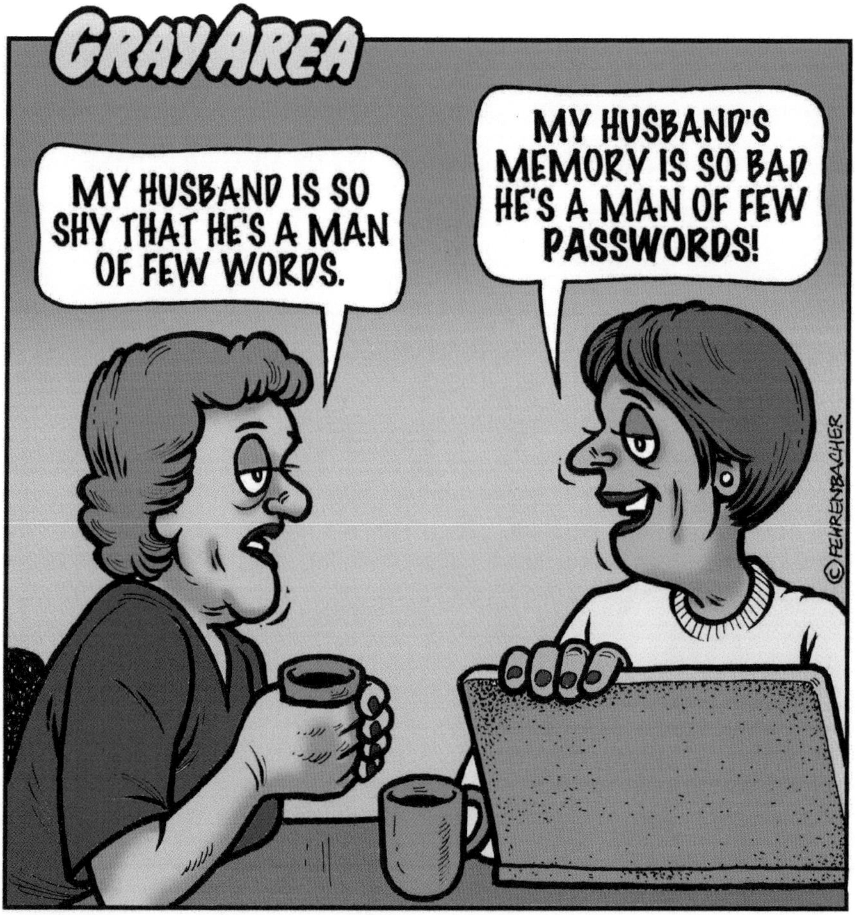
GRAY AREA
MY HUSBAND IS SO SHY THAT HE'S A MAN OF FEW WORDS.
MY HUSBAND'S MEMORY IS SO BAD HE'S A MAN OF FEW PASSWORDS!
© FEHRENBACHER

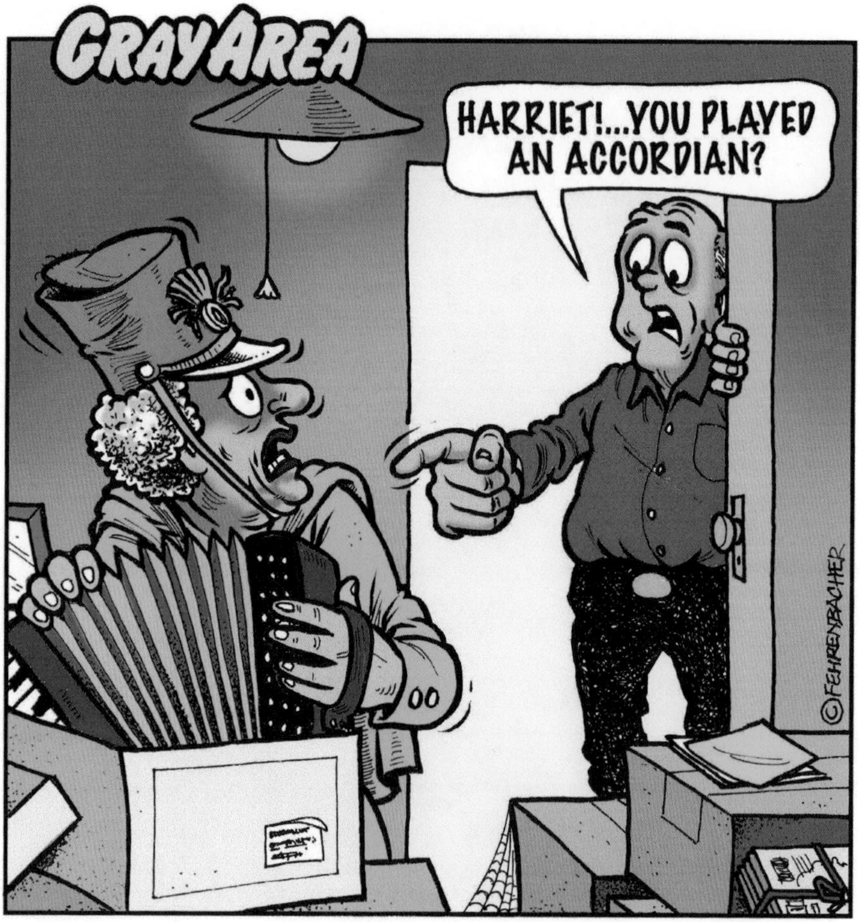
GRAY AREA
HARRIET!...YOU PLAYED AN ACCORDIAN?
©FEHRENBACHER

HARRIET COMES OUT OF THE CLOSET!

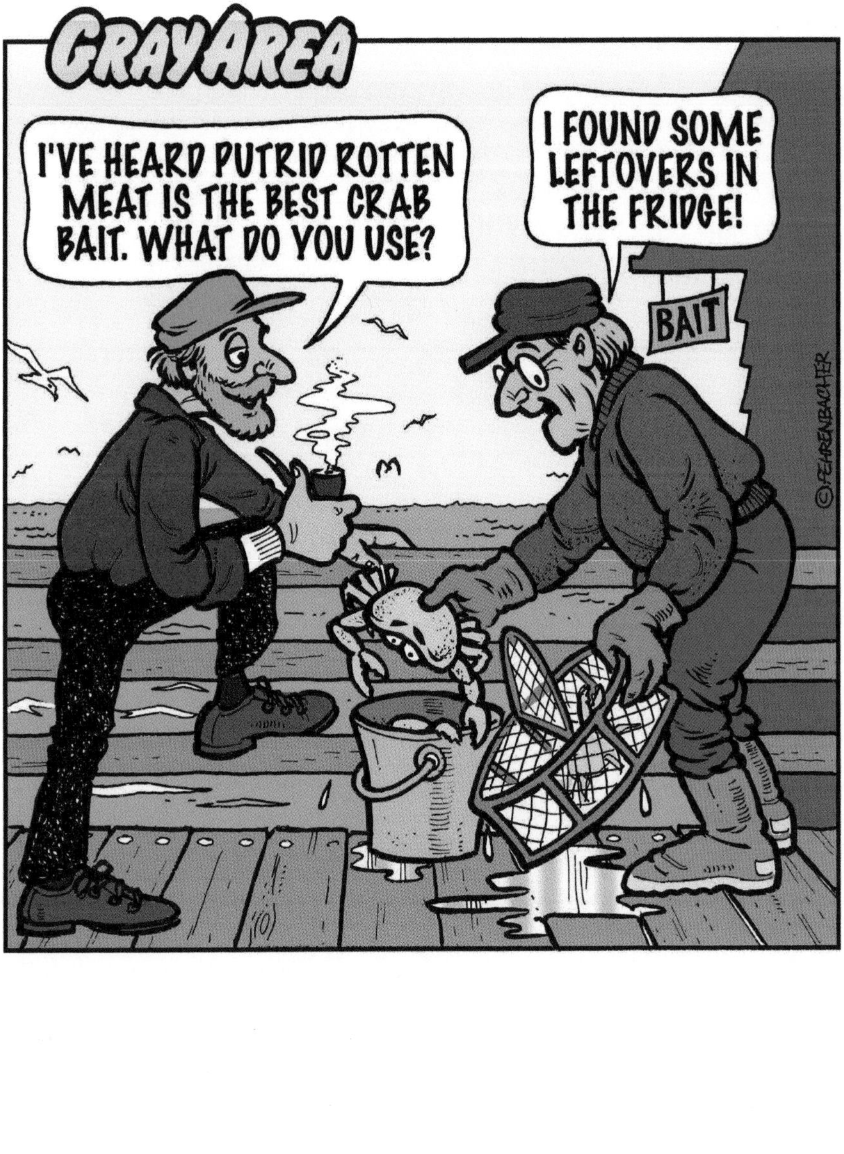
GRAY AREA
I'VE HEARD PUTRID ROTTEN MEAT IS THE BEST CRAB BAIT. WHAT DO YOU USE?
I FOUND SOME LEFTOVERS IN THE FRIDGE!
BAIT
©FEHRENBACHER

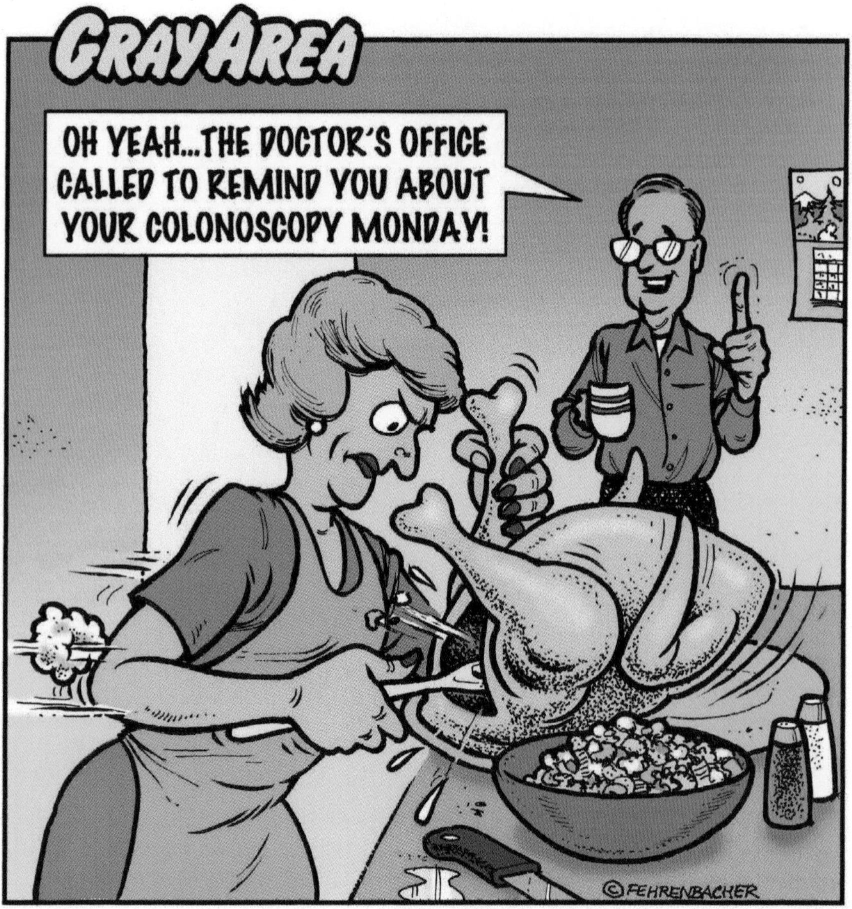
GRAY AREA
OH YEAH...THE DOCTOR'S OFFICE CALLED TO REMIND YOU ABOUT YOUR COLONOSCOPY MONDAY!
©FEHRENBACHER

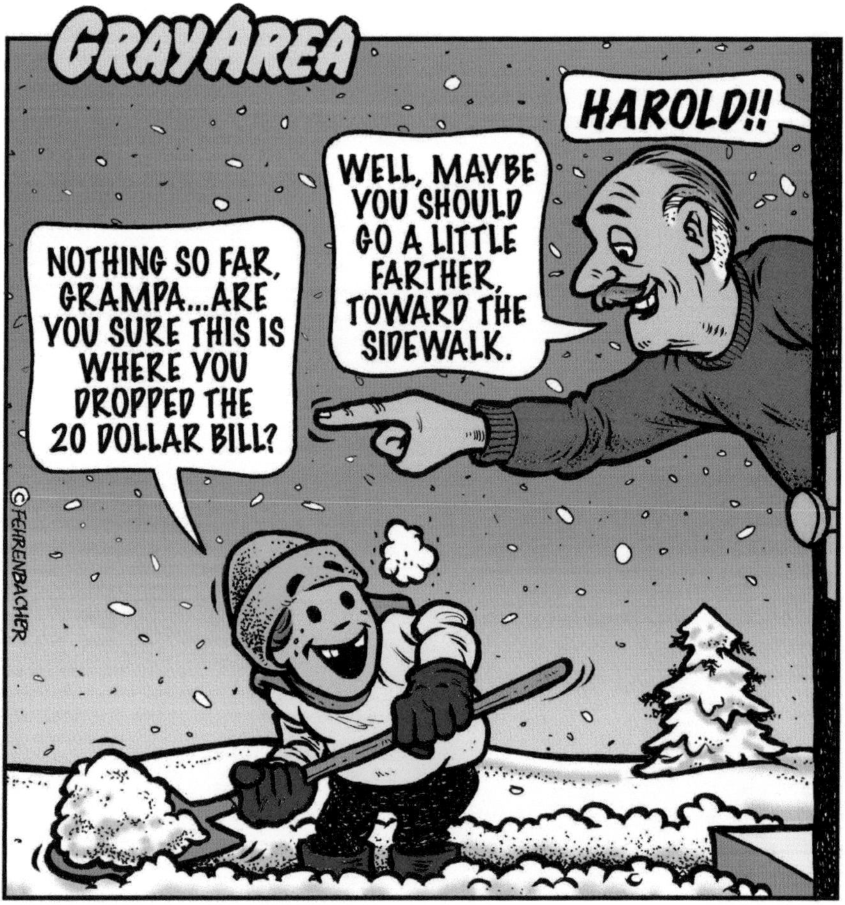
GRAY AREA
NOTHING SO FAR, GRAMPA...ARE YOU SURE THIS IS WHERE YOU DROPPED THE 20 DOLLAR BILL?
WELL, MAYBE YOU SHOULD GO A LITTLE FARTHER, TOWARD THE SIDEWALK.
HAROLD!!
© FEHRENBACHER

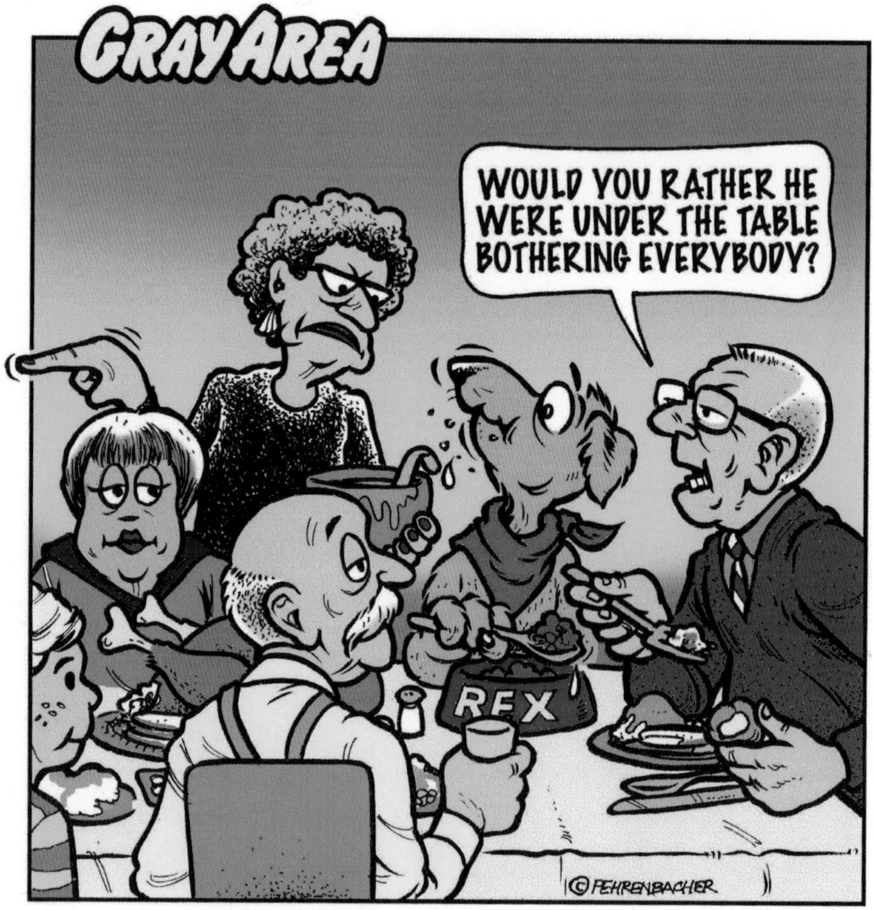
GRAY AREA
WOULD YOU RATHER HE WERE UNDER THE TABLE BOTHERING EVERYBODY?
REX
© FEHRENBACHER

HAVING THE "WHOLE" FAMILY FOR THANKSGIVING!

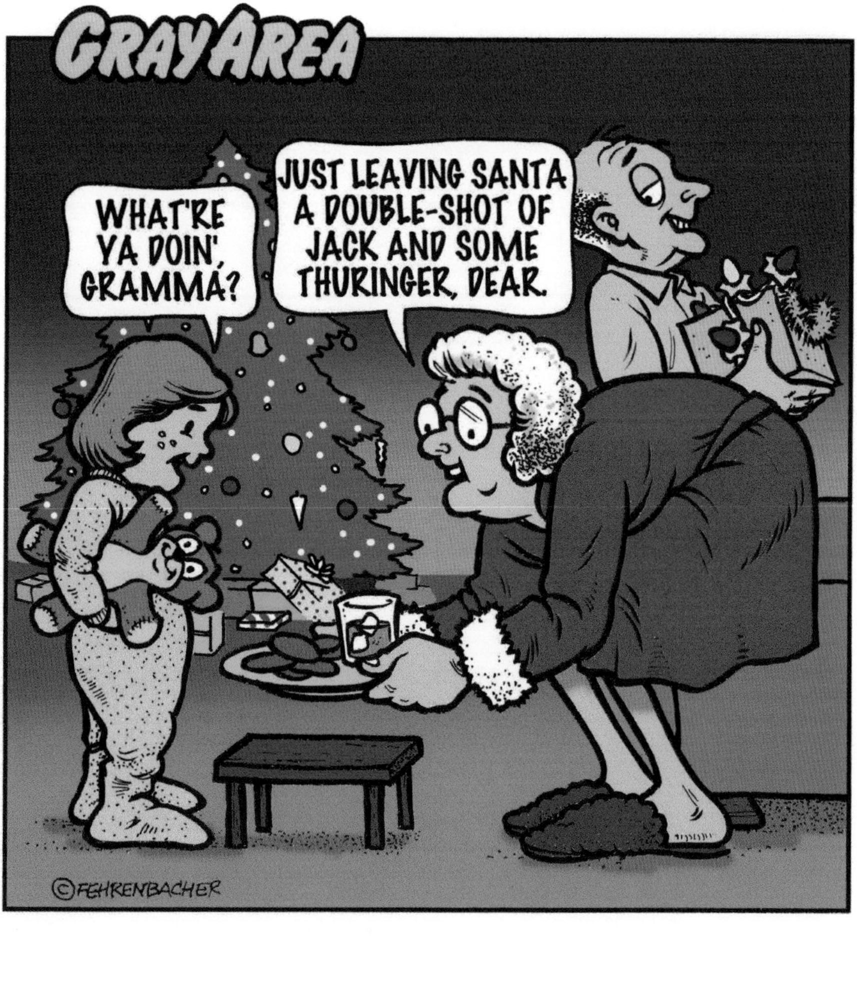
GRAY AREA
WHAT'RE YA DOIN', GRAMMA?
JUST LEAVING SANTA A DOUBLE-SHOT OF JACK AND SOME THURINGER, DEAR.
©FEHRENBACHER

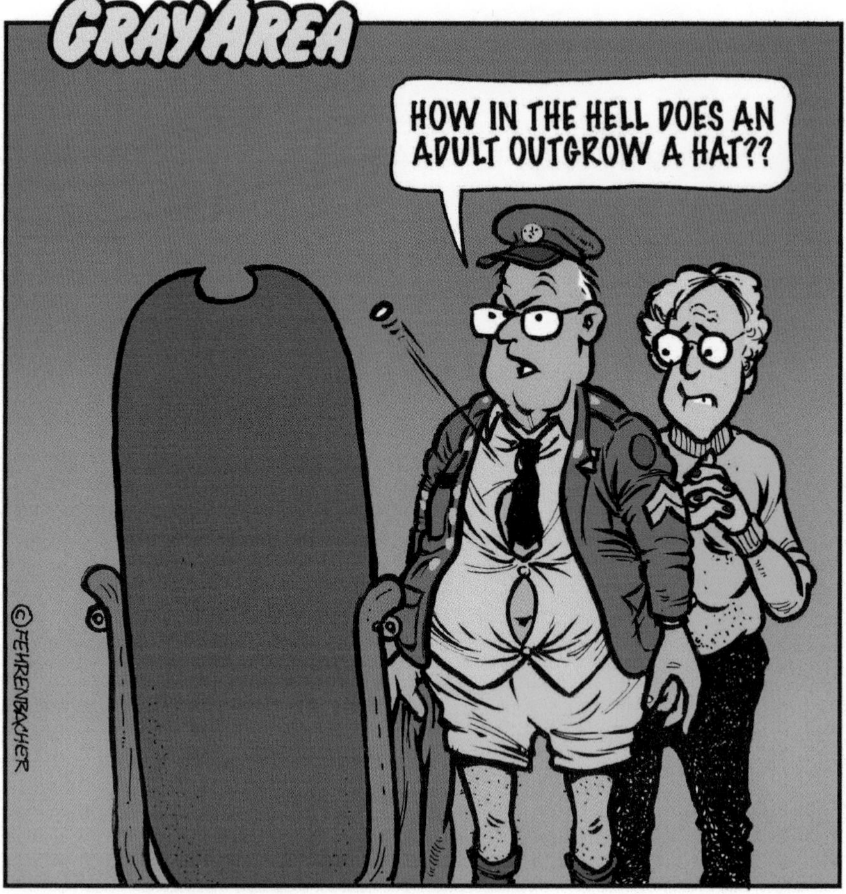
GRAY AREA
HOW IN THE HELL DOES AN ADULT OUTGROW A HAT??
© FEHRENBACHER

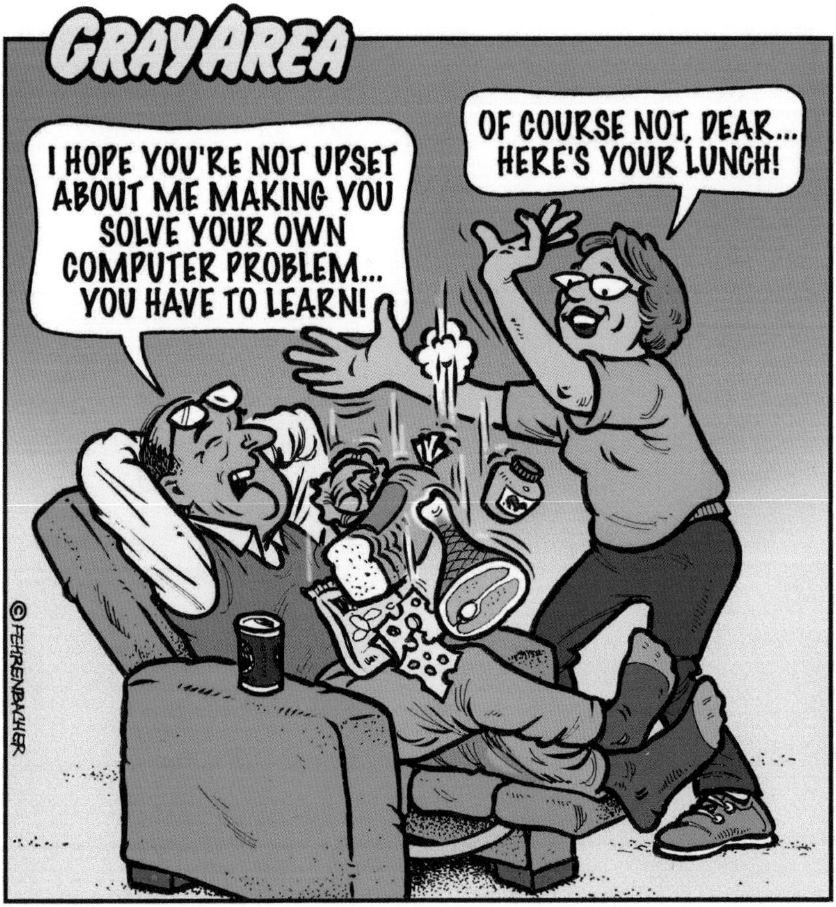
GRAY AREA
I HOPE YOU'RE NOT UPSET ABOUT ME MAKING YOU SOLVE YOUR OWN COMPUTER PROBLEM... YOU HAVE TO LEARN!
OF COURSE NOT, DEAR... HERE'S YOUR LUNCH!
© FEHRENBACHER

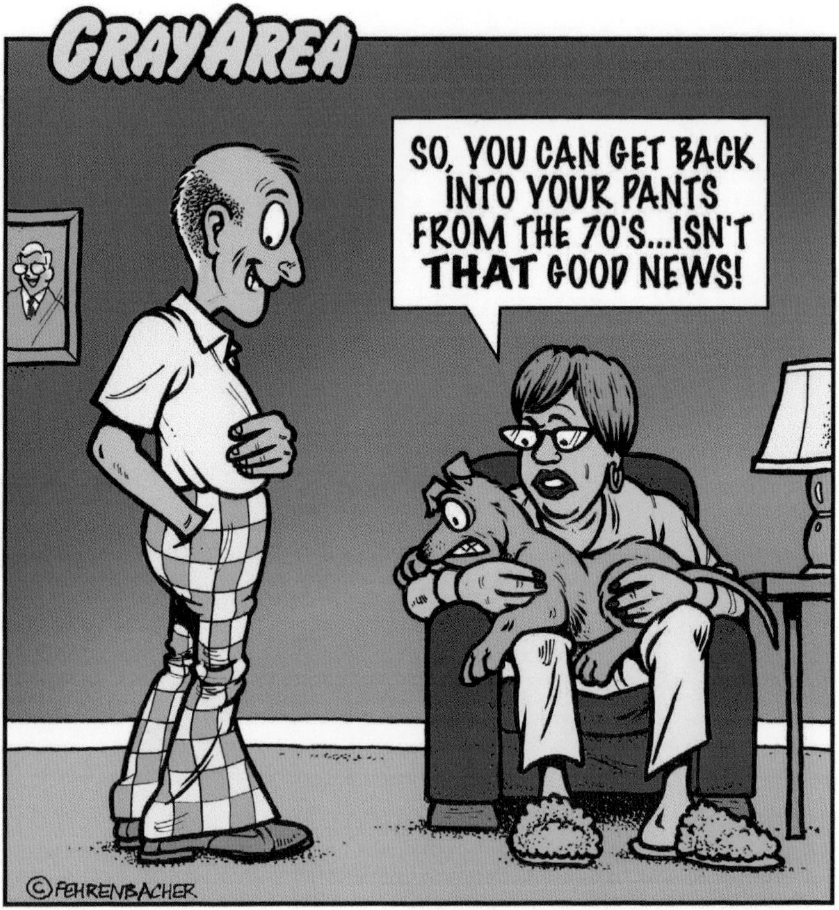
GRAY AREA
SO, YOU CAN GET BACK INTO YOUR PANTS FROM THE 70'S...ISN'T THAT GOOD NEWS!
©FEHRENBACHER

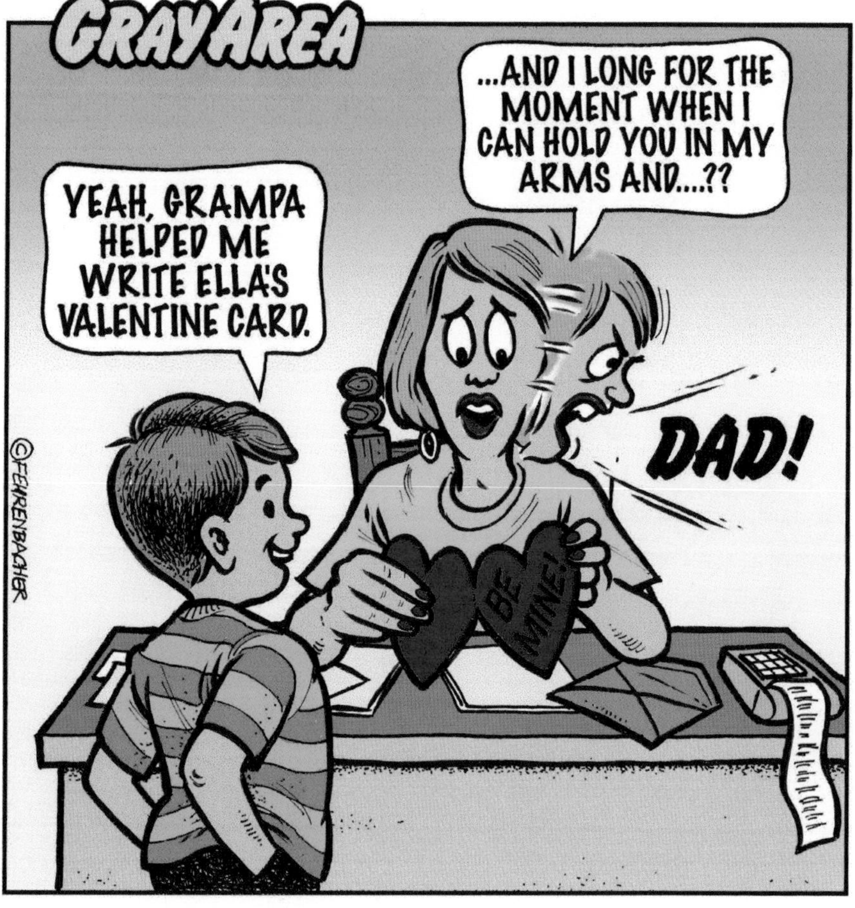
GRAY AREA
YEAH, GRAMPA HELPED ME WRITE ELLA'S VALENTINE CARD.
...AND I LONG FOR THE MOMENT WHEN I CAN HOLD YOU IN MY ARMS AND....??
DAD!
BE MINE!
©FEHRENBACHER

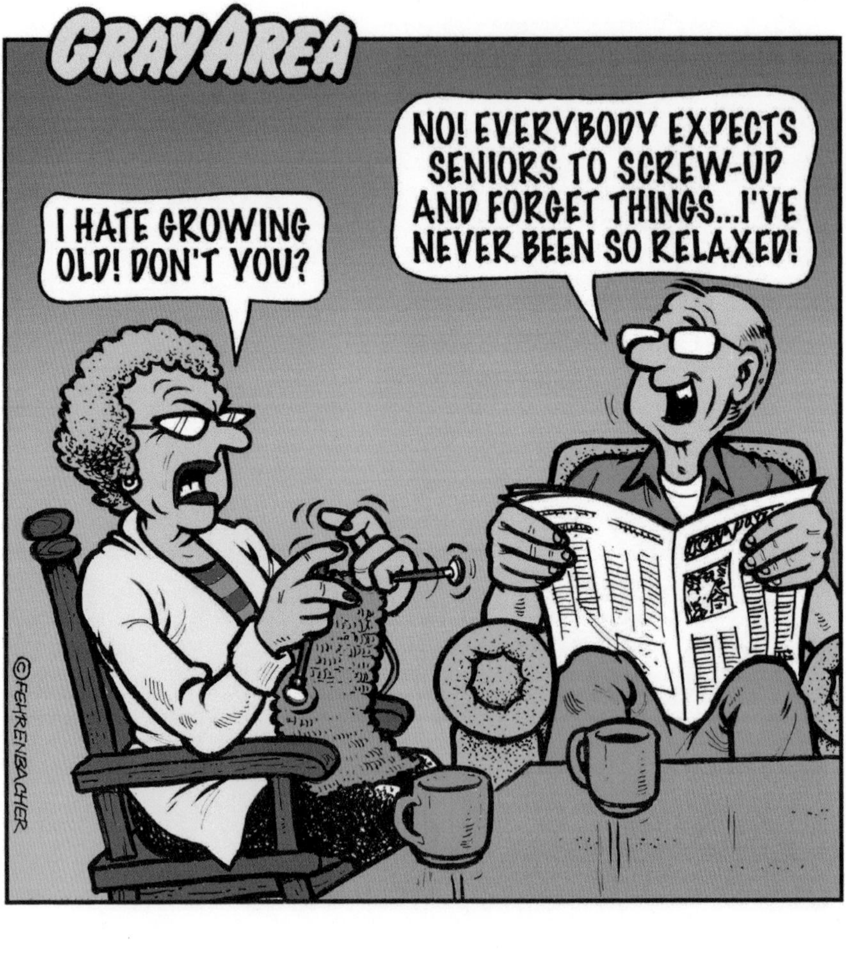
GRAY AREA
I HATE GROWING OLD! DON'T YOU?
NO! EVERYBODY EXPECTS SENIORS TO SCREW-UP AND FORGET THINGS...I'VE NEVER BEEN SO RELAXED!
©FEHRENBACHER

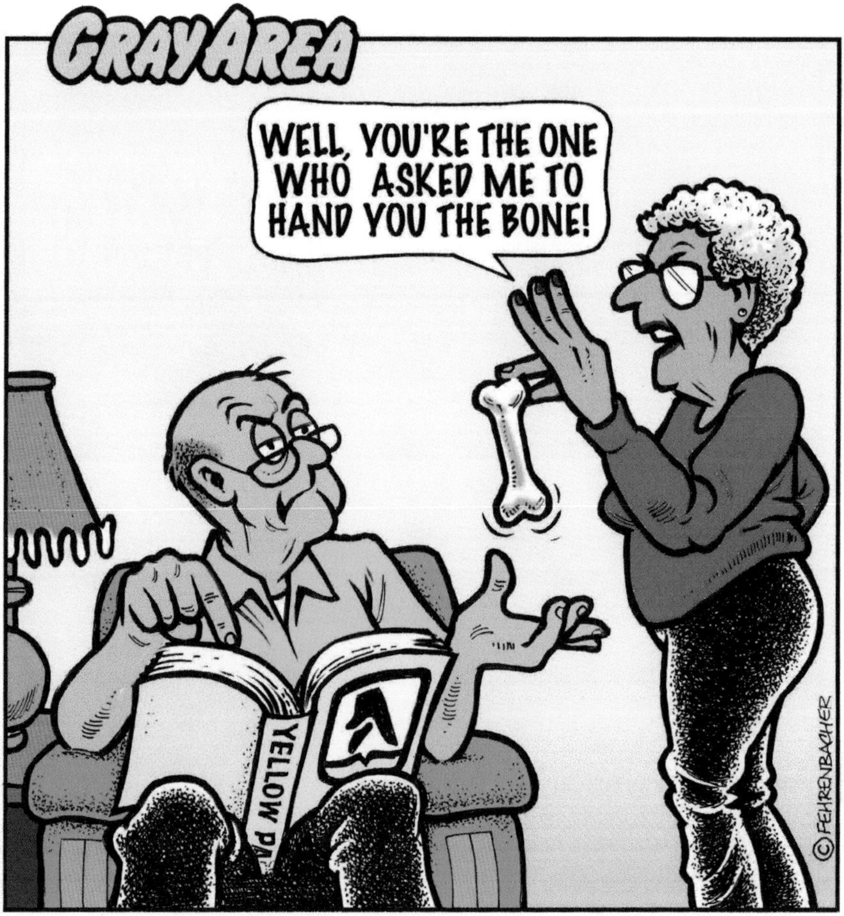
GRAY AREA
WELL, YOU'RE THE ONE WHO ASKED ME TO HAND YOU THE BONE!
YELLOW PA
©FEHRENBACHER

CAN YOU HEAR ME NOW?

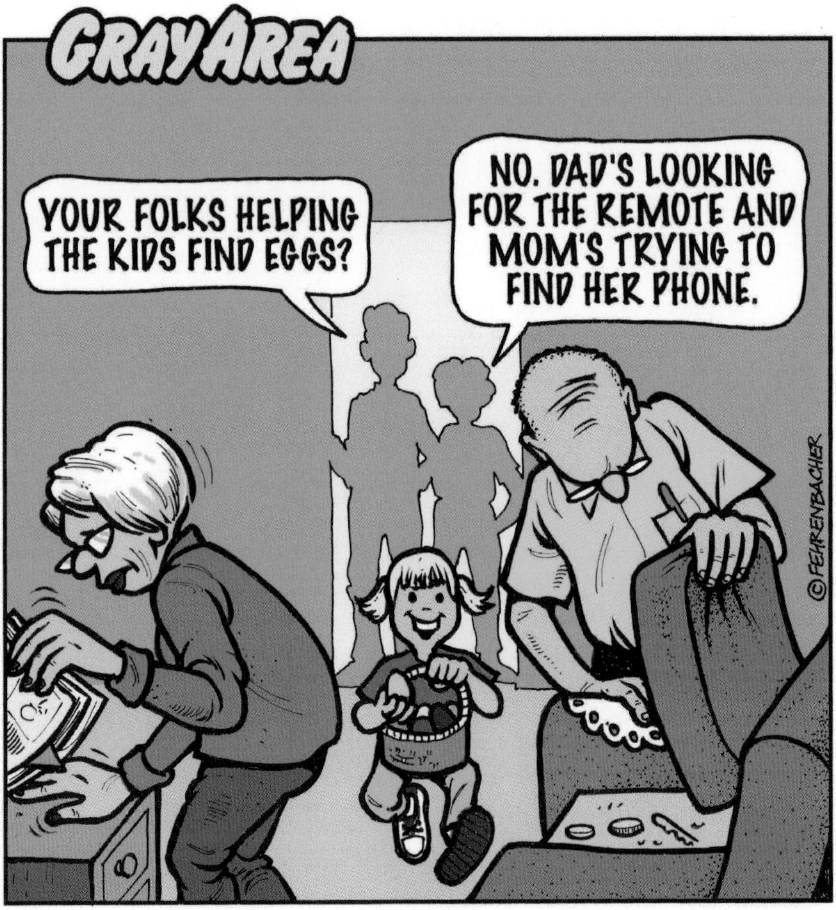
GRAY AREA
YOUR FOLKS HELPING THE KIDS FIND EGGS?
NO. DAD'S LOOKING FOR THE REMOTE AND MOM'S TRYING TO FIND HER PHONE.
©FEHRENBACHER

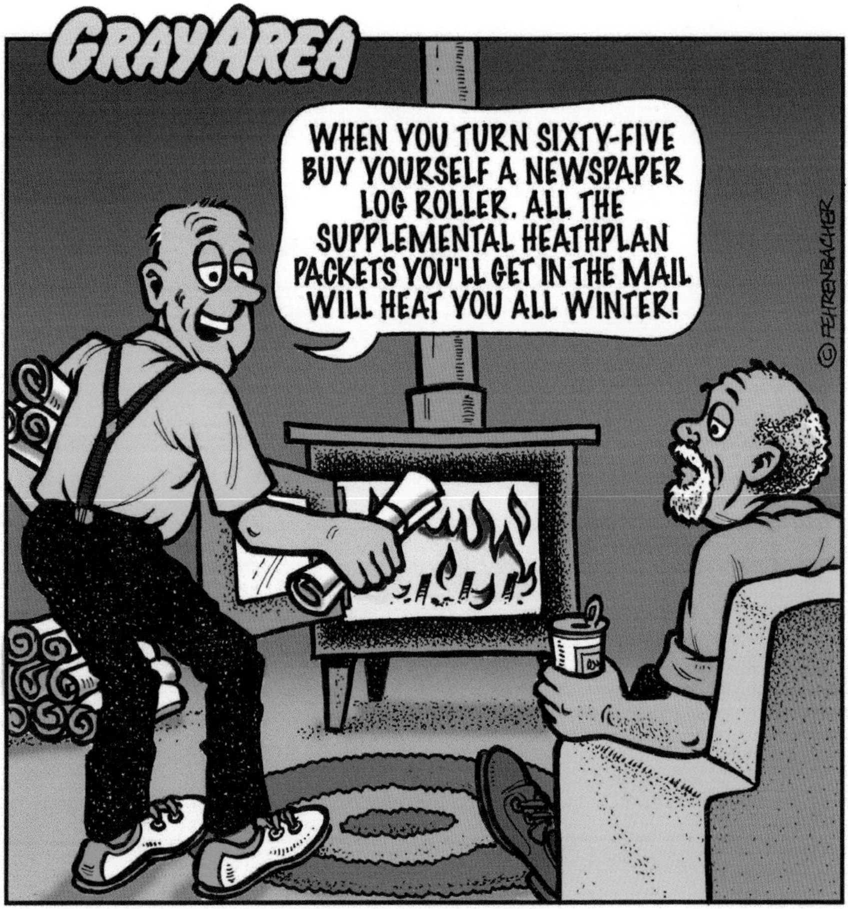
GRAY AREA
WHEN YOU TURN SIXTY-FIVE BUY YOURSELF A NEWSPAPER LOG ROLLER. ALL THE SUPPLEMENTAL HEATHPLAN PACKETS YOU'LL GET IN THE MAIL WILL HEAT YOU ALL WINTER!
© FEHRENBACHER

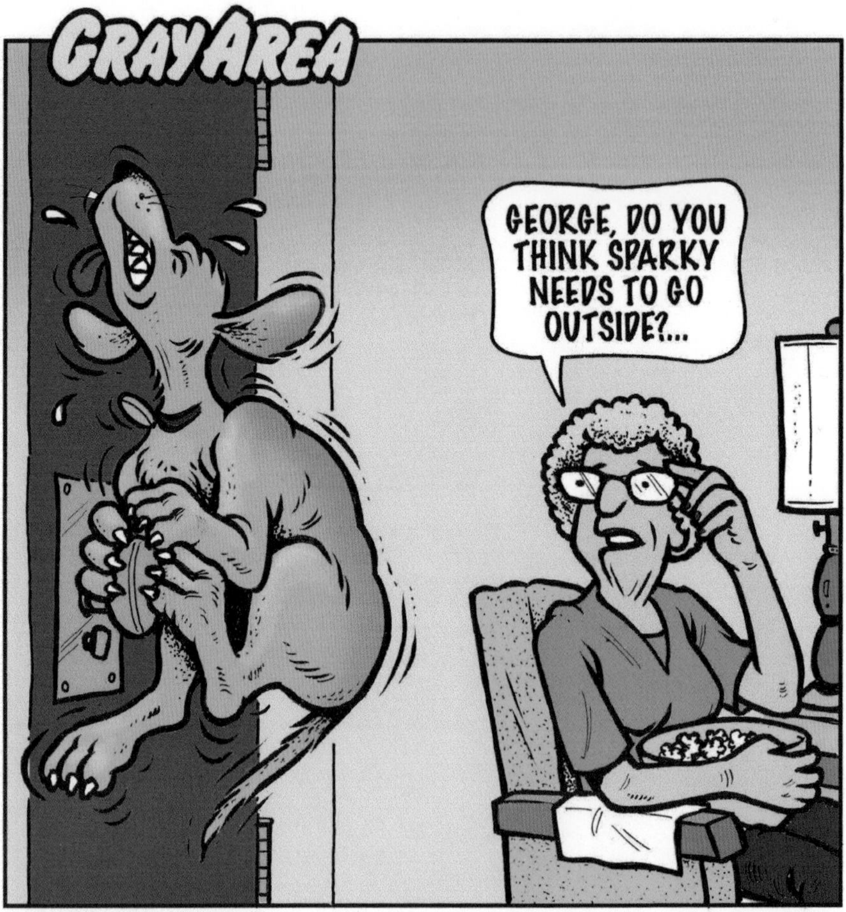
GRAY AREA
GEORGE, DO YOU THINK SPARKY NEEDS TO GO OUTSIDE?...

SENIORS LIKE TO GET A SECOND OPINION.

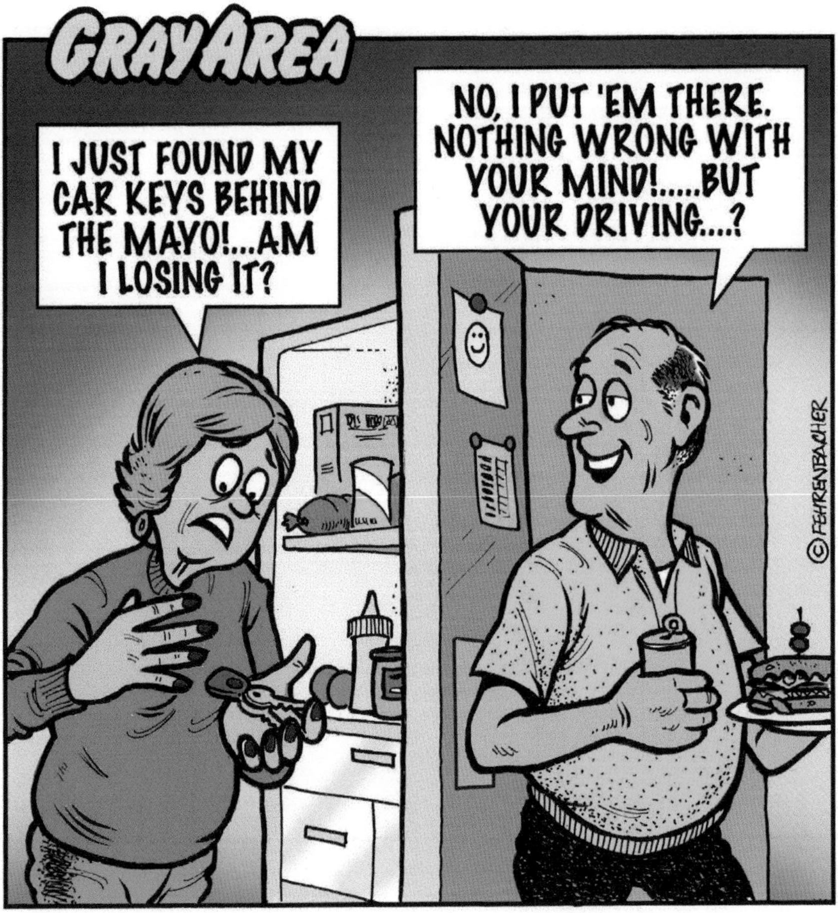
GRAY AREA
I JUST FOUND MY CAR KEYS BEHIND THE MAYO!...AM I LOSING IT?
NO, I PUT 'EM THERE. NOTHING WRONG WITH YOUR MIND!......BUT YOUR DRIVING....?
© FEHRENBACHER

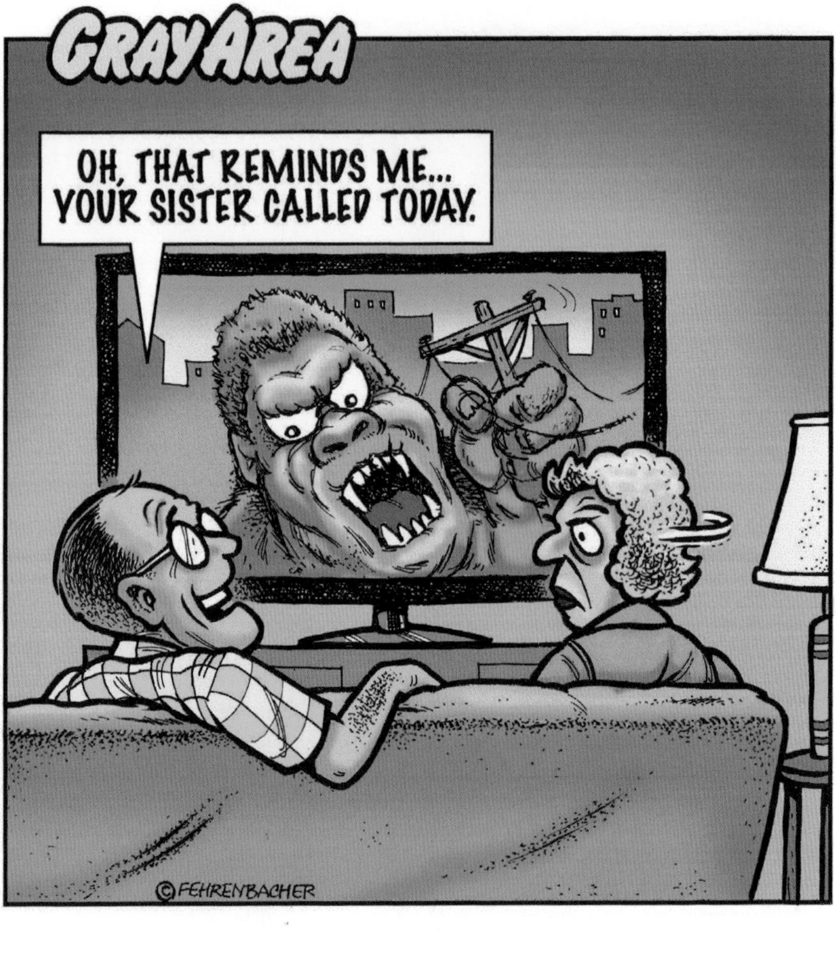
GRAY AREA
OH, THAT REMINDS ME... YOUR SISTER CALLED TODAY.
©FEHRENBACHER

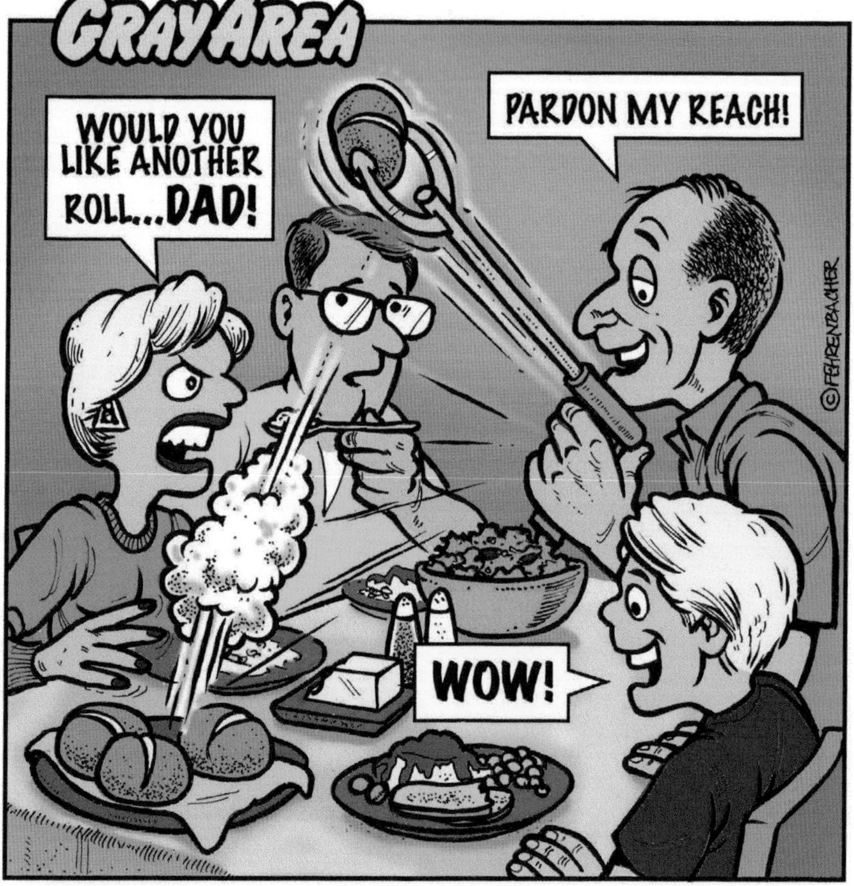
GRAY AREA
WOULD YOU LIKE ANOTHER ROLL...DAD!
PARDON MY REACH!
WOW!
©FEHRENBACHER

HAVING THE RIGHT TOOL FOR THE JOB.

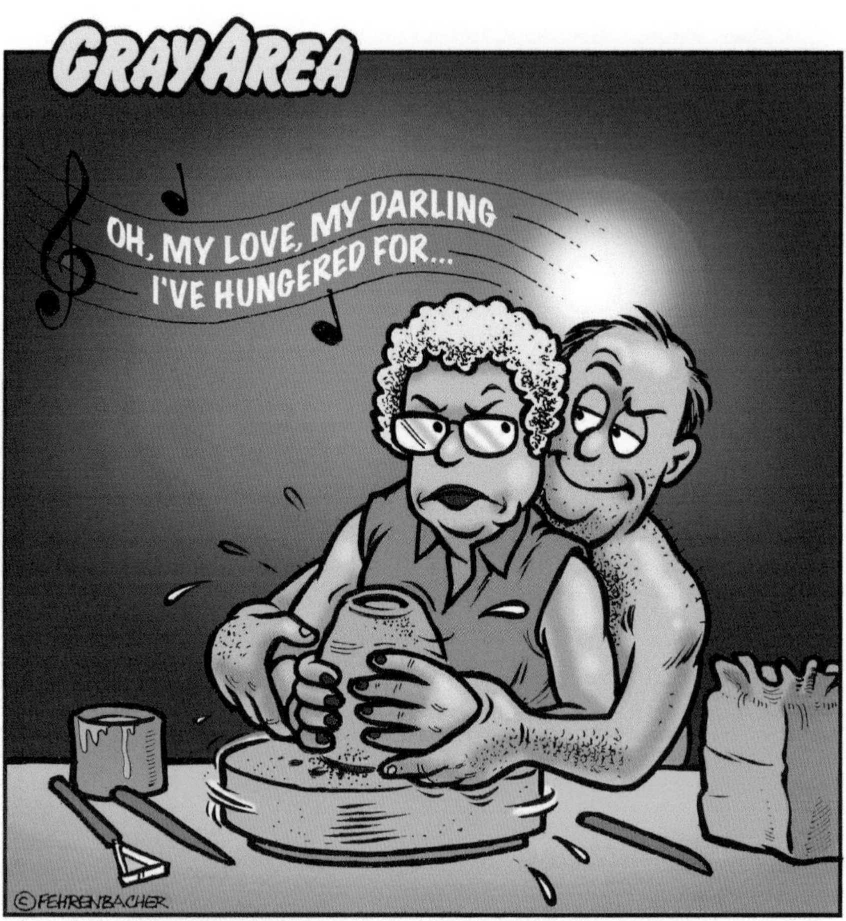
GRAY AREA
OH, MY LOVE, MY DARLING
I'VE HUNGERED FOR...
©FEHRENBACHER

GHOST..........OF A CHANCE!

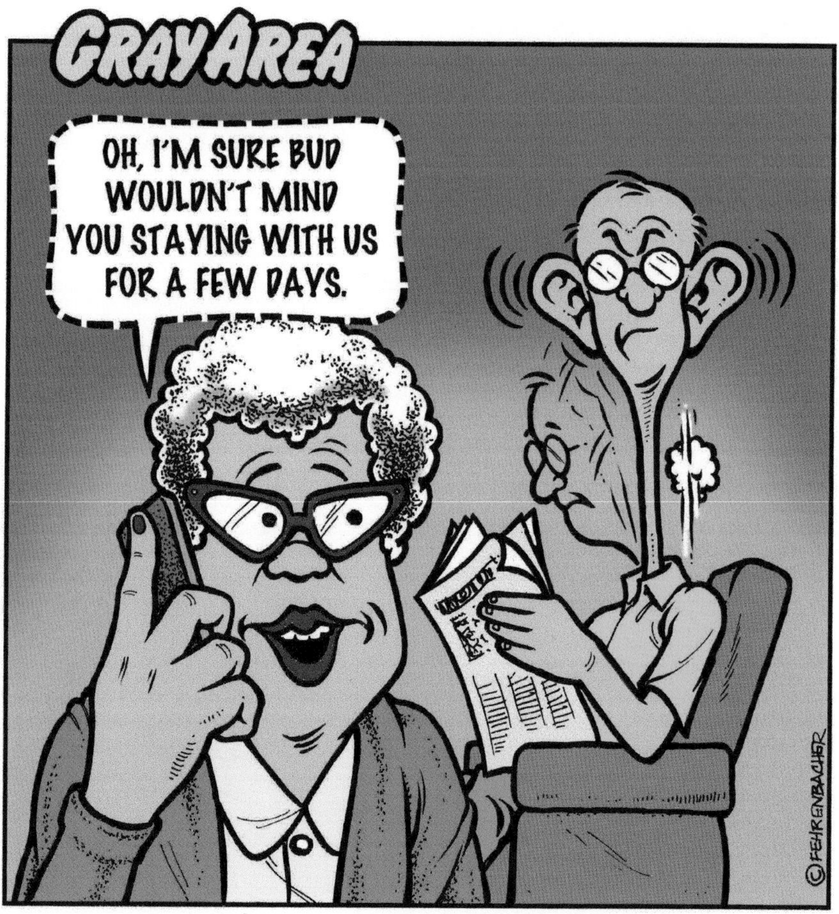
GRAY AREA
OH, I'M SURE BUD WOULDN'T MIND YOU STAYING WITH US FOR A FEW DAYS.
©FEHRENBACHER

SELECTIVE HEARING.

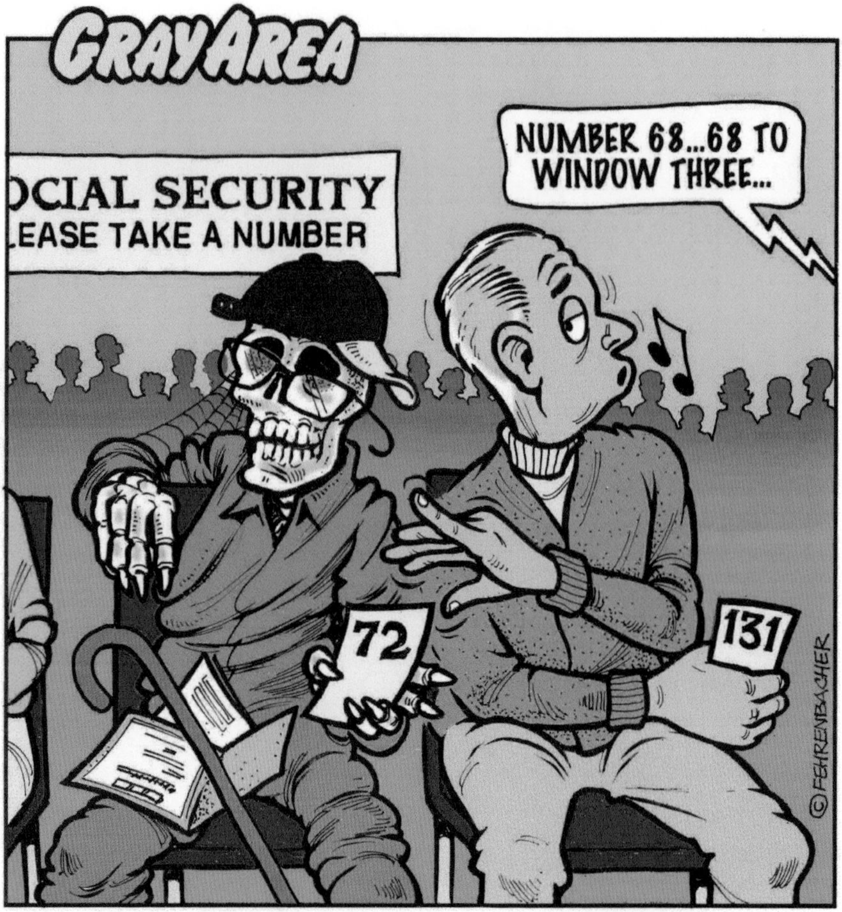
GRAYAREA
OCIAL SECURITY
LEASE TAKE A NUMBER
NUMBER 68...68 TO WINDOW THREE...
72
131
©FEHRENBACHER

RECOGNIZING AN OPPORTUNITY FOR ADVANCEMENT!

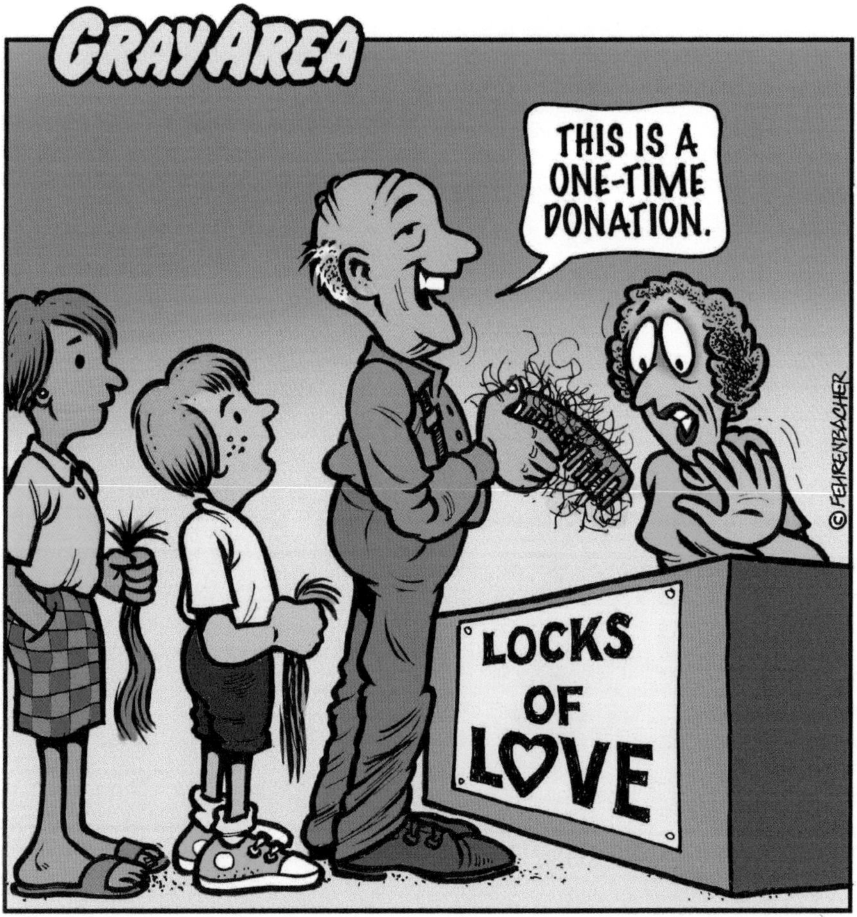
GRAY AREA
THIS IS A ONE-TIME DONATION.
LOCKS OF LOVE
© FEHRENBACHER

GIVING BACK TO THE COMMUNITY.

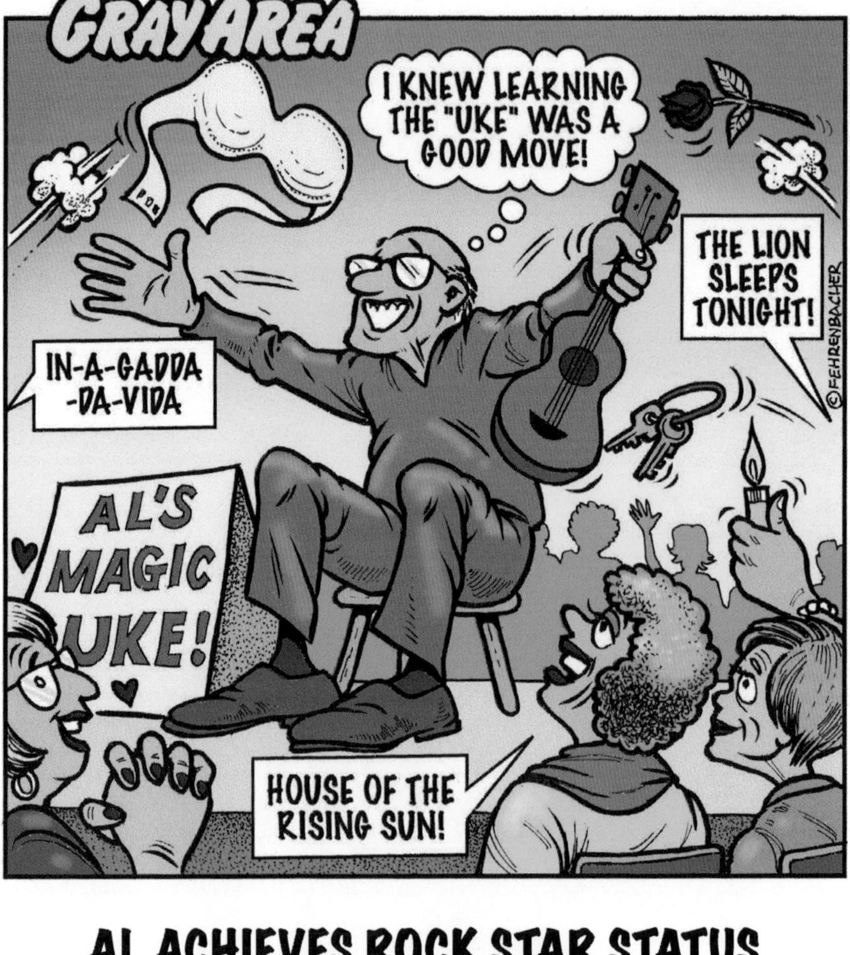
GRAY AREA
I KNEW LEARNING THE "UKE" WAS A GOOD MOVE!
THE LION SLEEPS TONIGHT!
IN-A-GADDA -DA-VIDA
AL'S MAGIC UKE!
HOUSE OF THE RISING SUN!
©FEHRENBACHER

AL ACHIEVES ROCK STAR STATUS AT THE HOME!

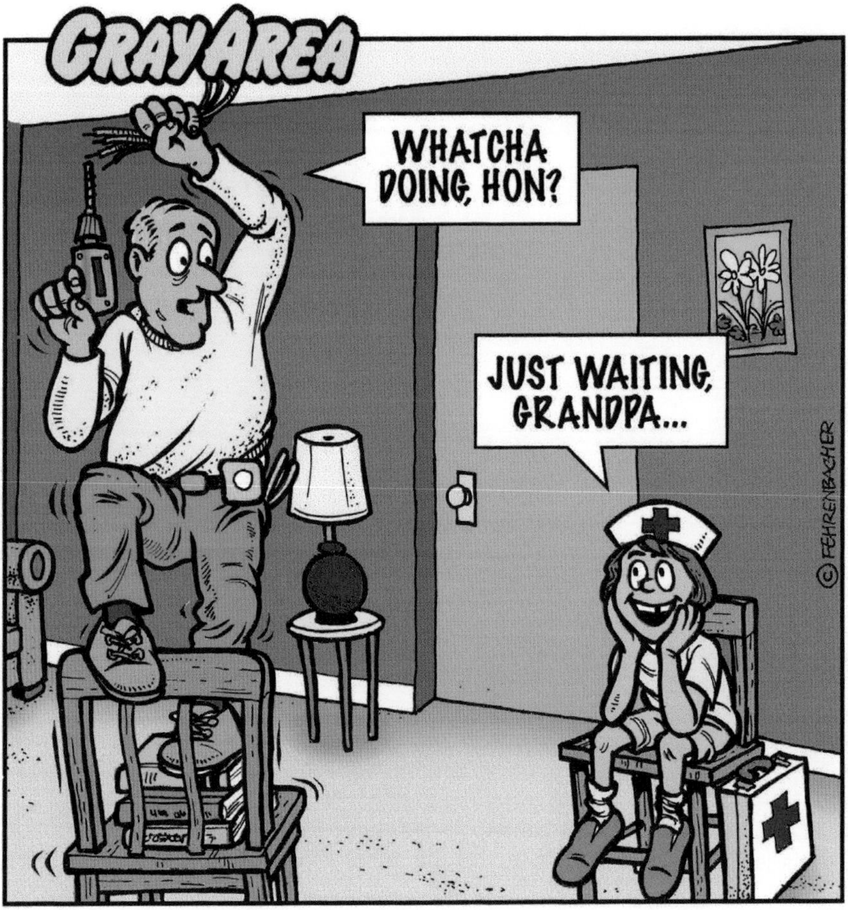
GRAY AREA
WHATCHA DOING, HON?
JUST WAITING, GRANDPA...
© FEHRENBACHER

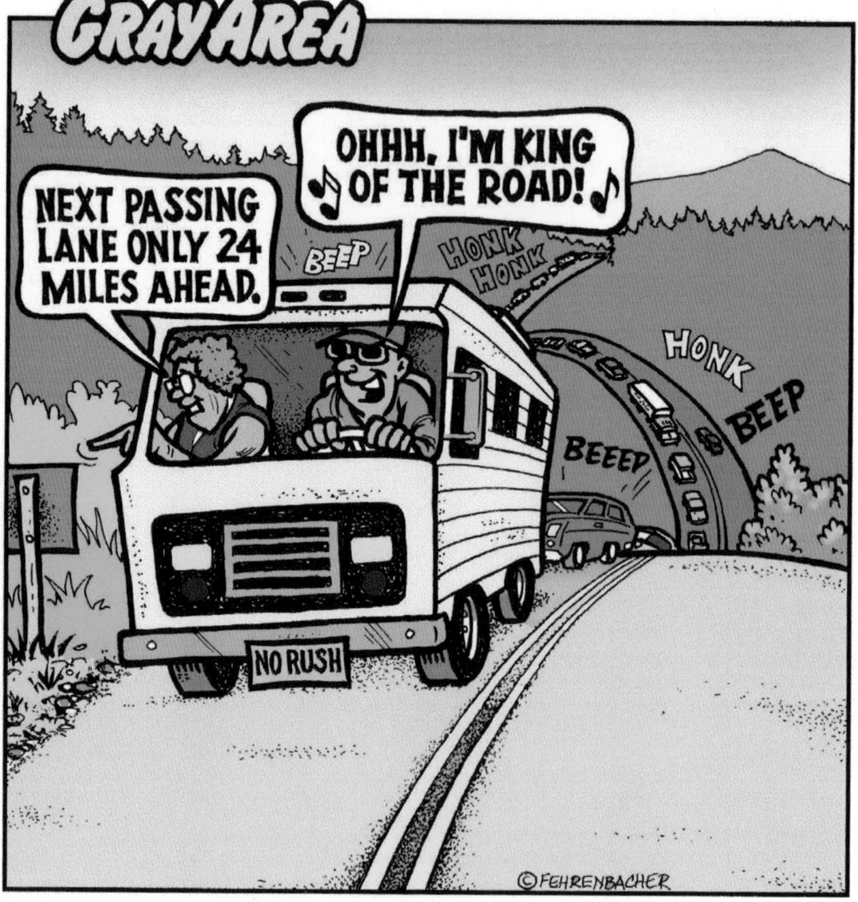
GRAY AREA
NEXT PASSING LANE ONLY 24 MILES AHEAD.
OHHH, I'M KING OF THE ROAD!
BEEP
HONK HONK
HONK
BEEP
BEEEP
NO RUSH
©FEHRENBACHER

LIFE IN THE "SLOW LANE!"

Printed in Great Britain
by Amazon